POLAND

A HANDBOOK IN INTERCULTURAL COMMUNICATION

POLAND

A HANDBOOK IN INTERCULTURAL COMMUNICATION

Eddie Ronowicz

National Centre for English Language Teaching and Research
Macquarie University, Sydney NSW 2109

Poland: A Handbook in Intercultural Communication

Published and distributed by
the National Centre for English Language
Teaching and Research
Macquarie University
Sydney NSW 2109

ISBN 1 86408 0663
ISSN 1036 1030

Typeset by DOCUPRO, Sydney.
Printed by Centatime Pty Ltd, Sydney
Cover design by Aahs International, Sydney.

*To my mother Doris
with many thanks for making sure
I was brought up as a bilingual.*

TABLE OF CONTENTS

PREFACE

Languages differ from one another not just as linguistic systems, but also as cultural universes.

(Wierzbicka 1985, p. 187)

Poland is a country where everything has a historical dimension. We are living, as it were, with the entire burden of our history on our shoulders, without being able to forget about the past, or to liberate ourselves from its omnipresent influence. This explains why history as a discipline is so popular in Poland: we have more than a hundred historical periodicals and the number of historical publications per year is close to 6000. Books on historical topics—not only historical novels but also memoirs and scholarly works—disappear immediately from the bookshops.

(Walicki 1990, p. 21)

In the early 1960s, when I was a university student in Warsaw, I had a phonetics lecturer who spoke English with excellent British pronunciation, and whose vocabulary and grammar were faultless. He had achieved this while studying in Poland and, even though he had been to Britain only on short visits, his command of English seemed to be that of a native speaker. After I had spoken to genuine native speakers of English, I realised there was something slightly peculiar about my lecturer's form of spoken English. It seemed 'too good to be true'. In fact, his pronunciation, stresses and rhythm were a perfect reproduction of Daniel Jones's Received Pronunciation, which is an idealised form of English created by averaging variants of the same sounds produced by native speakers. This form of spoken English is never spoken by native speakers, however well educated they may be, unless they make special efforts to do so. Thus, my lecturer's pronunciation was excellent for teaching purposes, but it was too perfect for everyday communication.

The lecturer in question also demonstrated other 'un-English' habits which very quickly betrayed his non-English background. For example, he would shake everyone's hand at the beginning of each meeting; when talking to English speaking people, he would stand uncomfortably close to them; and, despite encouragement to use first names when addressing his English friends, he insisted on using titles and family names. The professor thus behaved in a way that was acceptable within Polish culture, but was quite foreign to English ways. His knowledge of appropriate English cultural patterns did not match his language skills.

The lecturer is a clear example of a phenomenon that is often seen among language learners whose command of English may be very good, but who continue to behave according to the rules of their native culture. Because these are often markedly different from those observed by native speakers of English, the learners are often misunderstood. For instance, Polish tourists, business people and immigrants often have problems in communicating when they request, advise and discuss matters in a Polish manner, often sounding too direct and at times even rude. Unfortunately, this may have unfavourable consequences. For example, an English speaking employer who may not be aware that disrespect or impoliteness is not intended, may develop a negative attitude towards the Polish employee. The employee may not as a result be promoted or may be even dismissed because of what is considered by his employer to be inappropriate behaviour.

Poles residing in English speaking countries are constantly exposed to the communication patterns of native speakers of English and do usually learn these as they learn English. People who learn English as a foreign language in Poland, however, have to depend solely on their teachers and on written materials to acquire an understanding of these patterns. This is clearly not adequate. The best way to improve this situation is to use English language teachers who are familiar both with the attitudes, values and behaviours of Polish speakers and the cultural problems Poles may face when communicating with English speakers. It is also important to encourage the exploration of intercultural issues inside and outside the English language classroom. The Intercultural Communication series, of which this book is part, has been designed specifically for that purpose.

Poland: A Handbook in Intercultural Communication provides information on differences in patterns of linguistic behaviour in Polish and in English speaking cultures. It also encourages teachers and others working with Polish people to examine their own cultural assumptions and to identify areas where differences may cause difficulties. A series of activities designed to allow Polish learners of English to explore these areas are also included.

Background information is presented in the initial chapters to prepare the user for the study of specific topics later in the book. Some basic concepts of intercultural communication are discussed in Chapter 1. This is followed by background information on Polish history and society in Chapter 2 and a summary of most important grammatical differences between Polish and English languages in Chapter 3. The remaining chapters deal with some issues that affect cultural patterns of linguistic behaviour. Chapter 4 looks at the family and personal identity, while Chapter 5 deals with matters concerned with living in a society, including employment, housing, health and leisure. Chapter 6 examines such speech activities as requests, apologies and expressions of opinions. This is followed by a chapter on Polish attitudes to learning and teaching, and a chapter on Polish values. Chapter 9 looks at culture shock in the light of the Polish cultural experience.

Due to the fact that English is spoken as the first language in a number of countries, the question as to which culture should be taken as the basic model had to be decided at the very outset. In the end it was not only the fact that the book was written and published in Australia that determined the choice of that country as the model, but also the fact that Australian culture seems to have more in common with British and American cultures than the latter two have with each other. This is due to several factors. Britain was the source of a large number of immigrants to both the United States and Australia, and the source of the official language, English, used in these two countries. Unlike United States, however, Australia retained its political and cultural ties with Britain. The Queen is still the official Head of State of Australia, whereas United States has been totally independent of Britain for last 200 years. Consequently, Australia has not only taken in some of Britain's population, but has also inherited British institutions, system of education and the arts, as well as other cultural characteristics. Australia until 50 years ago was very much British. This changed after World War II when Australia established closer cultural and economic ties with the United States. These ties have been strengthened over time.

Thus, Australia shares a common language and a considerable common cultural core with both Britain and the United States. Texts and tasks within the texts based on Australian reality will, therefore, in most instances, require only minor adaptations for English students in most other English speaking countries.

The book has been designed for use in English language classes for Polish immigrants in English speaking countries, as well as in standard intermediate and advanced English language courses in Poland. The text is also a rich source of practical information for professionals, business people and government officials from both Poland and English speaking countries. I trust it will help people to avoid many pitfalls which can result from cultural misunderstandings.

Eddie Ronowicz

ACKNOWLEDGMENTS

Books such as this one tend to draw heavily on the experience, research and published works of others, many of whom cannot be specifically named because of limitations of space. In the bibliography I have listed the major sources used in this book, and quotations have been appropriately acknowledged. However, the numerous researchers and teachers who have contributed to my growing awareness of the problems of inter-cultural communication are too many to mention individually. I would like to thank them all. In particular, my thanks go to Professor Chris Candlin, who encouraged me to write the book in the first place, read the first draft and made extensive comments on a number of issues. I am also greatly indebted to Jean Brick, the editor of the Intercultural Communication series. Her friendly encouragement and advice, as well as ideas on the teacher and student questions have contributed significantly to the final result. I also extend warm thanks to Nada Madjar whose copy editing skills were highly valued.

I would like to thank a number of my Polish and Australian friends who read the first draft of the manuscript and shared their reactions with me. Specifically, I would like to thank Maria Lipiec, a social worker among Polish immigrants in Sydney, whose remarks proved to be particularly useful in preparing the final version of the book. My thanks also go to Laura Klos Sokol, a sociolinguist at Warsaw University, who gave me the manuscript of her book in which she has described her firsthand observations of cultural differences between Poles and Americans. It provided me with invaluable insights into the way Poles are perceived by native speakers of English.

Finally, I would like to thank my wife and children for their support, patience and undertstanding they showed me while I was writing the book.

LIST OF MAPS

CHAPTER ONE

LINGUISTIC AND CULTURAL ASPECTS OF COMMUNICATION

Language and Communication

Communication is one of the most important aspects of our everyday life. There are different ways in which people can communicate, but natural verbal languages—as opposed to artificial languages such as those of computers—are the most frequently used. This is because they are the most efficient way of transmitting messages between people.

From the linguistic point of view, a natural language is a communication tool made up of a list of words (vocabulary) and a system of rules governing their use (grammar). If every word in the vocabulary was to have only one unchangeable meaning and the grammar consisted of a limited number of fixed rules, then to communicate effectively participants would simply have to be competent in the use of one list of words and one set of grammatical rules. This indeed is the case with artificial languages, but not so with natural languages which have vocabularies and grammars that can be used to produce almost unlimited number of original messages. As Corder (1973) points out:

> No one knows 'the whole' of any language, or how to use it appropriately in all possible situations of language use. He acquires those parts of it which he needs in order to play his part in society. As he grows older, the roles that are ascribed to him or that he acquires change and develop, and as they change he learns more of his language (he may also forget some). (p. 201)

Since using a language involves knowledge as well as choice of vocabulary and grammatical patterns, not all native speakers of a given natural language use all registers with equal fluency. As linguistic research has shown, an average adult native speaker uses only a small proportion of the available vocabulary.

How much of a language's potential then do people who are learning it as a second language use? Migrant children who begin to learn a language in their early teens or earlier can reach the same level of competency as average native speakers, provided they are exposed to it soon after arrival. They may need to attend special language classes to catch up, especially if they have already completed the initial grades of the primary school, but otherwise they will acquire English naturally. Adult immigrants and those who learn English as a foreign language in their native country, on the other hand, tend to learn the language mainly in the classroom. This does not necessarily put them at a disadvantage, for many of them achieve a remarkably high standard within three years. The problem is, however, that language competence alone is not enough to communicate successfully, for language itself is but a code which functions within the framework of its culture. Learners, therefore, must be able to combine their language competence with an awareness of the accepted norms of the community within which that language is used.

Culture and Communication

When two people who speak different languages have problems in communicating, it becomes immediately obvious that the problem is a lack of a common language. The difference in cultural norms which underlie linguistic behaviour are, however, not so easily discerned.

Culture in its broadest sense is a comprehensive view of a society's history. It encompasses politics, economics, social history, philosophy, science and technology, education, the arts, religion and customs, which can be studied either as they have developed over a long period of time in history or as they are or were at a given point in time. Culture includes the spiritual aspect of a society, embracing its ideological, artistic and religious trends. It is also its everyday life, including day-to-day activities, entertainment, fashions, living conditions, family and social relations, customs, beliefs, morality, behavioural patterns and rituals. Social consciousness is also part of culture expressed in the language, as are social values, art, institutions and organisations of a given society. It is 'seemingly permanent, yet constantly changing' reality (Suchodolski 1986, p. 5) which is ever-present to all individuals belonging to the same cultural group.

The political, social and economic history of a given cultural group, as well as its spiritual heritage can be learned about fairly easily from books. To understand the complex reality of its everyday life and social consciousness, however, is much more difficult. In order to do this, the learner must become familiar with a multitude of culture-specific patterns of communication and the more recent social, cultural, political, economic and spiritual history of the community. Because adult members of a language community participate in events, have access to the local media and constantly communicate with other people in their community, they share a store of information built over many years, which they use in everyday communication. Not surprising then, foreign visitors and immigrants, even if they know the language well, find it difficult to comprehend much of the contents and many of the references used by native speakers.

The most problematic areas are humour (especially political jokes), metaphors and references to the not-so-distant past of a particular community. For instance, the famous statement by the former Australian Federal Treasurer, Paul Keating, about 'the recession we had to have' became part of everyday language in Australia, but barely made the news elsewhere. Consequently, people who have come to Australia after that time probably find it hard to understand why most Australians find the phrase amusing even when it is used in a serious context.

Traditions and present-day events influence the ever-changing vocabulary and idioms of a language, linguistic patterns and choice of elements of the past which are considered relevant to the life of a particular language community. Successful communication, therefore, depends not only on phonetic and grammatical correctness, but also on an understanding of the context, when, where and how things should be said or whether they should be said at all.

For example, Klos Sokol (1994) points out, that while Americans find even short stretches of silence a tortured eternity when in the presence of other people, '. . . among Poles, it's acceptable that people not have something to say every second of time spent together—a rather intimate notion' (p. 43). Klos Sokol illustrates this point with the following incident:

> During a dead-still traffic jam, I sat in a car with a Polish friend who fell silent, obviously irritated with our immobility. I felt compelled to fill up the weighty silence with lively and entertaining chatter. But since I was tired and grumpy too, my noble efforts resulted in empty blather. She finally turned to me and said gently, 'If you don't feel like talking, you don't have to.' Caught! Red-handed! Making filler small talk. It would have been okay to say nothing.
> (p. 43)

Native speakers of a particular language normally choose an appropriate way of delivering their message because they have the same basic knowledge of the history and traditions of their community. This knowledge is constantly updated. Furthermore, they acquire during their formative years a repertoire of cultural rules which are firmly linked to the language. These cultural rules allow members of a common culture to modify their linguistic behaviour according to the requirements of a given situation. Speakers of other languages likewise follow a set of cultural rules, which are different from the rules of other cultures. Consequently, problems of intercultural communication arise.

People usually take linguistic and cultural rules of communication for granted and tend to assume that all other people operate within the same system. For example, when, in an English speaking environment one native speaker says to another, 'Shut the window, Mr Johnson.', it would most likely be intended as a joke, indicated by the very formal address. If, however, this was said in the same situation but by a Pole, it would be an error resulting from the Polish person's assumption that Polish cultural norms of formal address can be translated into English. More often than not however, the participants would not realise that there was miscommunication and a misunderstanding would result. It is for this reason that the teaching of intercultural communication needs to be and integral part of all English language programs.

Culture Shock

People usually do not realise how much their daily life is influenced by unwritten rules, which are automatically accepted and applied by their social class, neighbourhood or country, until they move into another culture. It is only then that they realise they have problems in interpreting other people's behaviour and that the assumptions which have guided their behaviour at home are no longer applicable. In short, they realise that the new social environment follows a different set of rules, some of which may be very difficult to comprehend. In most cases this leads to culture shock—a phenomenon experienced by most people who move from one culture to another.

According to Brick (1991):

> Culture shock is the result of the removal of the familiar. Suddenly the individual is faced with the necessity of working, commuting, studying, eating, shopping, relaxing, even sleeping, in an unfamiliar environment, organised according to unknown rules. In mild form, culture shock manifests itself in symptoms of fatigue, irritability and impatience . . . Some people may respond by developing negative stereotypes of the host culture, by withdrawing as much as possible from contact with host-country nationals, by refusing to learn the language and by mixing exclusively with people of their own cultural background. In extreme cases, rejection may be so complete that the individual returns immediately to their own culture, regardless of the cost in social, economic or personal terms. (p. 9)

For an adult, culture shock can be an excruciating experience, leading to feelings of disorientation, frustration and helplessness. This is especially true of immigrants and people on long contracts in a foreign country. On arrival, they usually have a positive attitude towards their stay, but they soon find that the ways they used to do things at home are not always acceptable in the host country, where people not only speak a different language but often seem to behave in strange and unexpected ways.

Almost all new arrivals experience some form of culture shock. Its intensity and duration depend on a number of personal and social factors, the most crucial one seeming to be the degree of difference between the familiar and the new environment. This, as Kalantzis *et al.* (1986, pp. 112–18) point out, may not necessarily be the difference between two distinct national cultures, but rather the difference between two environments. For instance, a Polish miner from Katowice would probably adjust much better to living in the New South Wales mining community of Maitland, than a Scottish farmer would to living in New York.

The tendency of immigrant groups to form ghettos in the host countries such as Australia, Canada, England and the United States has been well documented (Pakulski 1985, p. 99 ff; Smolicz & Secombe 1985, p. 110). In Australia, recent surveys of native language maintenance and use among first generation migrants (Smolicz & Secombe 1985; Clyne 1991) confirm that these ghettos indeed do exist. Post-Solidarity emigrants who came to Australia in the early 1980s, for instance, have not formed visible enclaves, but they nevertheless continue to live in cultural ghettos by socialising mainly with other Poles, cultivating Polish traditions and showing little interest in establishing contacts with Australians and adopting Australian culture. This is irrespective of their proficiency in English and successful employment.

One possible reason why such ghettos are created is the immigrants' inadequate understanding of cultural patterns of communication in English and their inability to use these patterns correctly. This may lead to continued feeling of alienation from the mainstream society, making it more difficult for immigrants to overcome the inevitable culture shock. This also suggests that while a marked increase in the level of English competency helps immigrants significantly to adapt to their field of work, failure to address the cultural issues results in limited integration.

Most people eventually overcome the initial difficulties. They usually go to work, mix with other people and learn the new ways. They also come into contact with various institutions and thus gradually learn how to operate successfully in the new environment. However, language learners often find that the process of adaptation into the new society is slow and difficult, mainly because little attempt is made to examine the cultural attitudes underpinning linguistic communication. It is very important, therefore, to make the study of intercultural communication a part of all English teaching programs.

1. Have you ever spent a long period of time in a country other than your own?
2. Which aspects of your stay did you find most pleasant and rewarding?
3. Did you experience any of the symptoms of culture shock? What were they? How did you cope with them?
4. Have you ever noticed any behaviour by your students that might indicate they are experiencing culture shock? Describe some of these behaviours.
5. What do you think you can do to help your students deal with culture shock?

Teaching Intercultural Communication

Today's English language courses have moved a long way from the traditional approach of presenting the cultural component of a language in the form of excerpts from literary masterpieces or texts describing important historical and cultural events. The traditional approach provided the students with little or no information on contemporary life of English speaking people or practice in everyday language. As a result of research undertaken since the 1950s, the modern concept of teaching language for communication has now been firmly established. Most modern English courses today teach the language contextually and many follow functional and notional syllabuses, which include information and exercises on culturally determined patterns of language behaviour.

The main aim of standard English courses, however, is still to teach pronunciation, spelling, vocabulary, grammar and listening, reading, speaking and writing skills. The main difference between the more recent and older teaching materials is that vocabulary and grammar are no longer taught by using long quotations from literature or endless repetitions of isolated sentences. Rather, they are taught in the context of everyday situations with illustrations of different types of social encounters in which the vocabulary and structures can actually be used. Nevertheless, the cultural context of language is still left largely unexplored.

This presents difficulties even at elementary levels. For example, one of the first lessons in most language courses focuses on asking and answering questions about peoples' names. The appropriate vocabulary and grammatical structures are taught, but what is often not taught is the culturally appropriate way of addressing people, which is a very sensitive area of intercultural communication. The stage is thus already set for intercultural miscommunication.

The situation becomes even more serious at more advanced levels. As learners' language competency and ability to participate in genuine communication grows, they are increasingly exposed to situations in which comprehension and responses depend as much on understanding of and ability to use appropriate cultural patterns as on the mastery of English grammar and vocabulary. The more advanced the learners' English, the more they will be expected by native speakers to respond in a culturally appropriate manner. While new learners are likely to be forgiven for violating cultural norms, those who are perceived as being more fluent are more likely to be seen as being deliberately impolite.

About This Book

This book has been written to avoid just such miscommunication. It is designed for use in regular language programs or for teaching separate specialist courses. It can also be used by language teachers wishing to deepen their understanding of their Polish students, by those in service organisations who work with Poles, by business people and, indeed, by anyone who has dealings with Polish people.

Each chapter includes questions and activities designed to help readers examine their cultural assumptions and to compare them with the assumptions of others. They have been developed on the basis that learning involves doing as much as knowing.

This book, and the Intercultural Communication series, is based on Australian experience. Although historical experiences of Britain, Canada, the United States and New Zealand have resulted in the emergence of different English speaking cultures from that of Australia, this book can be used equally well in any one of these countries. Readers are encouraged, however, to use the questions and activities in each chapter to explore the differences between the English speaking cultures, as well as differences between these and Polish culture. The term 'English speakers' as used in this book refers to those who, regardless of their ethnic background or place of birth, have been socialised into a culture which traces its roots back to an Anglo-Celtic past.

Polish readers are encouraged to use every opportunity to interact with native English speakers. However, they may often have no choice but to rely on English language teachers or use texts to obtain information. The bibliography at the back of this book provides some suggestions for further reading.

In conclusion, it needs to be pointed out that the aim of this book is not to turn

Poles into 'true-blue Australians' or any other nationality, for it may not be of benefit to erase all traces of their original culture. In fact, learners need to have cultural choices rather than the inflexibility of operating only in one system. Rather, the aim of this book is to help the learners to understand culturally determined aspects of communication and to respond to them appropriately. When they achieve that, they will be able to choose the extent to which they wish to conform to these patterns. They will be in a position to make informed choices about the language they use, rather than unwittingly create unintended impressions.

> In your view, to what extent should the issues of culture shock and cross-cultural adjustment be addressed in language classrooms?

Things to Think About

What advice would you give to a friend contemplating moving to a different country?

CHAPTER TWO

BACKGROUND
Polish History and Society

Polish History

Poland appeared on the map of Europe for the first time in the 10th century AD. This was as a result of military and political exploits of Mieszko, the chief of the Polanie tribe which inhabited the territories between the Wisła and the Odra rivers. At the time Poland was a comparatively small country, but by the end of the 14th century, after it was united with Lithuania, Poland was a large commonwealth. At the end of the 18th century, it was annihilated by its three neighbouring powers, Austria, Prussia and Russia. Thereafter, Polish history has largely been a story of defeat and internal failure.

Founding and Expansion of Poland

The traditional founding date of the Polish state is 966, the year the ruler of the Polanie tribe Prince Mieszko I was baptised and thus made his people part of the family of Christian European nations. Due to a lack of written records, little is known about Mieszko's predecessors, except that before Mieszko there were several con-secutive rulers from the same Piast family. They must have contributed significantly to the gradual territorial expansion and increasing strength of the tribe.

Soon after the Polish state was founded its territories were expanded further under the rule of Mieszko's son, Bolesław the Brave, who began a strong push towards the east. This was at the cost of losing some of the western provinces along the Odra River, which were not returned to Poland until after World War II.

In turning his attention to the east, Bolesław began the expansion which eventually made Poland one of the European powers. Unfortunately, later this was also to prove one of the main reasons for Poland's downfall. Bolesław's conquests and cunning political maneuvers were rewarded towards the end of his life, when in 1025 he became the first crowned King of Poland to be officially acknowledged by Rome.

The Piast Dynasty ruled Poland until 1370. The initial period of building and strengthening the kingdom was interrupted in the 13th century, when King Bolesław Krzywousty divided the kingdom into regions. These were to be governed by his five sons, the eldest of whom was to be the senior ruler. A period of disintegration and chaos followed, caused by conflicts between members of the Piast Dynasty. This ended at the end of the 13th century when Prince Władysław Łokietek began to reunite Poland. For over 30 years Władysław Łokietek expanded his control over the territories, until he eventually controlled most of the regions. He was crowned the King of Poland in 1320.

Władysław Łokietek's son, Casimir the Great, is considered by many to have been the greatest Polish ruler. During his reign (1333–70) foundations were laid for Poland to become a great power. The central government was strengthened, the administration of the country was reformed and roads and bridges were built. In 1364 Casimir established in Cracow the first university in Central Europe, which in time became a centre of learning of European renown.

Like his predecessors, Casimir was keen to expand his territories towards the east. This ambition was realised 16 years after his death when Poland and Lithuania were united by the marriage of Queen Jadwiga, a descendant of the Piast Dynasty, and the Lithuanian Duke Władysław Jagiełło. This was the beginning of a new Polish dynasty, the Jagiellons.

The union of the two kingdoms was established to oppose pressure from the Germans in the west and the Teutonic Order to the north. After the joint Polish and Lithuanian forces defeated the Teutonic Order at the battle of Grunwald in 1410, the Commonwealth of Poland and Lithuania became the greatest power in that part of the world, lasting for the next 400 years. In 1569 Poland and Lithuania entered a more permanent political union. They now had one king and equal privileges were given to both Poles and Lithuanians.

The growth of the Polish-Lithuanian Commonwealth during the 15th century was matched by impressive cultural developments during the 16th century, known as the 'Golden Age of Polish Culture'. The University of Cracow (now the Jagiellonian University) became an international centre of learning, excellent literature was produced in Latin and Polish, and other forms of art were developed. During the Reformation and the Counter-Reformation, Poland was a haven of religious tolerance, where many nationalities of various religious persuasions lived in harmony.

The Golden Age was the peak of Poland's development and, at the same time, the beginning of its disintegration. This was caused mainly by the power of the nobility (*szlachta*) which limited the power of the king, and the sheer size of Poland's territory, which had been over-expanded to the east. When Sigismund August, the last of the Jagiellons, died without an heir in 1572, Polish monarchy became elective, thus opening it to rivalry between various European courts. This form of monarchy also gave the nobility, who were to be the electorate, even greater powers.

The Polish nobility came mainly from the ranks of the knights and soldiers who accompanied the kings of the Piast and Jagiellon dynasties. They were given privileges and land in return for exploits on the battlefield. By the time of Casimir the Great, they were a distinct social class of land owners whose main duty was to be available for military service in time of war. Because they were virtually the only source of the king's power, the nobility gradually acquired more privileges, including an ever-increasing influence on important state decisions. By the time the last of the Jagiellon monarchs died in 1572, all the nobility, irrespective of their personal wealth, were considered equal. They had power to make most important state decisions by themselves, first at *sejmiki* (local gatherings) and at rallies of nobility, which were later transformed into the national *Sejm* (Diet). Their power was confirmed by the Nihil Novi Constitution of 1505, which stated that 'nothing new can be decided in state matters without the consent of the diet'.

Consequently, the elected kings who reigned during the next two centuries had very little actual power. Their election to the throne and subsequent activities were controlled by the nobility, as were all important state decisions. The situation was made worse by various internal and external forces and richer noble families (the magnates) who began to bribe the less wealthy nobles so that certain proposals would be put forward and the bribed nobles would vote as the wealthy noble families wished. All this caused the central administration of the commonwealth to gradually disintegrate.

During the first 400 years of Poland's existence the territory under the monarch's control contracted and expanded according to the internal political situation and the success and failure of military campaigns. However, the general push toward the east continued until Poland was united with Lithuania. From a relatively small country at the end of the 10th century, the kingdom grew into a Polish-Lithuanian Commonwealth. During the 16th and 17th centuries, Poland was the largest state in Europe, stretching from the Baltic Sea in the north to the Black Sea in the south, and with the eastern border stretching beyond the Dnieper River.

The Disintegration of the Polish-Lithuanian Commonwealth

In times of peace and in the absence of powerful neighbours, Poland was not difficult to govern and its borders were easily protected. However, Poland became very vulnerable during the 17th century when its external conditions changed. While the Polish-Lithuanian Commonwealth was enjoying the benefits of the union and its conquests, three of its neighbours began to grow rapidly. The Austrian Empire,

Figure 2.1 Territorial expansion of Poland from the the 10th to 17th centuries.

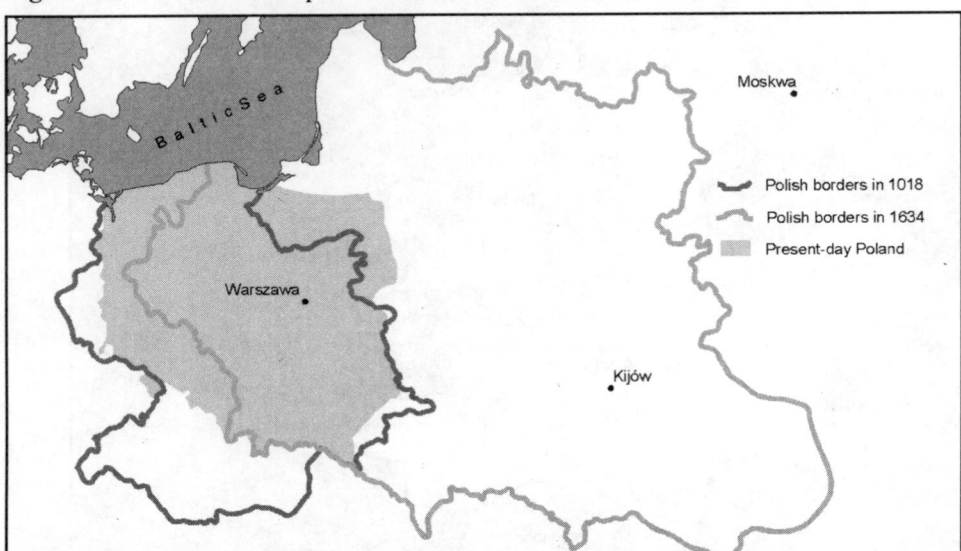

bordering Poland in the south and southwest, grew into a formidable power as a result of royal marriages. East Prussia, which had been defeated by Poland in the 15th century, also grew in strength during the 16th century, and in 1701 was joined by Brandenburgia and a number of other German territories to form Prussia. Poland thus became vulnerable along its northern and western borders. Finally, the Principality of Muscovy in the east began to expand rapidly towards the end of the 15th century, culminating at the beginning of the 18th century in the creation of the powerful Russian Empire by Peter the Great. Thus, by the beginning of the 18th century, Poland was surrounded by powerful neighbours who set the scene for its destruction.

The 17th century was marked by internal and external wars which devastated large areas of Poland and contributed to the erosion of its central power. At the same time, the Polish military force, despite some spectacular victories—such as the victory of the Polish King Jan Sobieski over Turkish forces which ended their siege of Vienna in 1683—was becoming outdated. By the turn of the 18th century most European countries had regular armies, while Poland still retained the old system of calling on its nobility to form the army in times of war. This system had worked very well when Poland was smaller and when the commonwealth was enjoying times of relative peace. However, Polish army thus formed was no match for the well trained and disciplined armies of Austria, Prussia and Russia, which already in 1697, a year after Sobieski's death, were in a position to impose upon the electorate Augustus II of Saxony as the next King of Poland.

The first half of the 18th century Poland was ruled by the Saxon Dynasty. This was a period of further disintegration, marked by increasing political influences of

Figure 2.2 Poland and its neighbours before the first partition in 1772.

its three powerful neighbours. In 1764 Catherine the Great, the Empress of Russia, secured the election to the Polish throne of the pro-Russian Polish noble, Stanisław August Poniatowski. Soon afterwards Prussia and Russia began a campaign to protect the 'rights' of Orthodox and Lutheran minorities in Poland. In response, a group of Polish nobles rebelled against the king. This led to the first partition of the commonwealth in 1772, as a result of which Poland lost almost a third of its territories and half of its population.

After this first partition Poland finally realised that its very existence was seriously threatened. Consequently, a reform movement was organised by the Polish nobility, which led to the adoption of a new Constitution by the *Sejm* (Diet) on 3 May 1791. Hereditary monarchy was re-established, obsolete laws were changed and new ones introduced to make Poland a modern state. Included among the measures was the establishment of a regular professional army. The changes, however, came too late to prevent the final collapse of Poland. The Constitution (known as the 3rd of May Constitution) in fact was responsible for the military invasion by Russia in 1792 and the second partition of Poland by Prussia and Russia in 1793.

The Polish nobility—the traditional defenders of the country—made one further effort to save the country from total annihilation. An attempt was made by Tadeusz Kościuszko to organise an armed insurrection, but because he did not get sufficient support from the mass peasant population, the uprising was defeated by the Russian forces under General Suvorov. The third and last partition of Poland, in which all the three neighbouring powers took part, occurred in 1795. Consequently, Poland was completely wiped off the map of Europe and did not appear again as a fully independent country until the end of World War I.

Figure 2.3 The partitions of Poland in 1772, 1793, 1795.

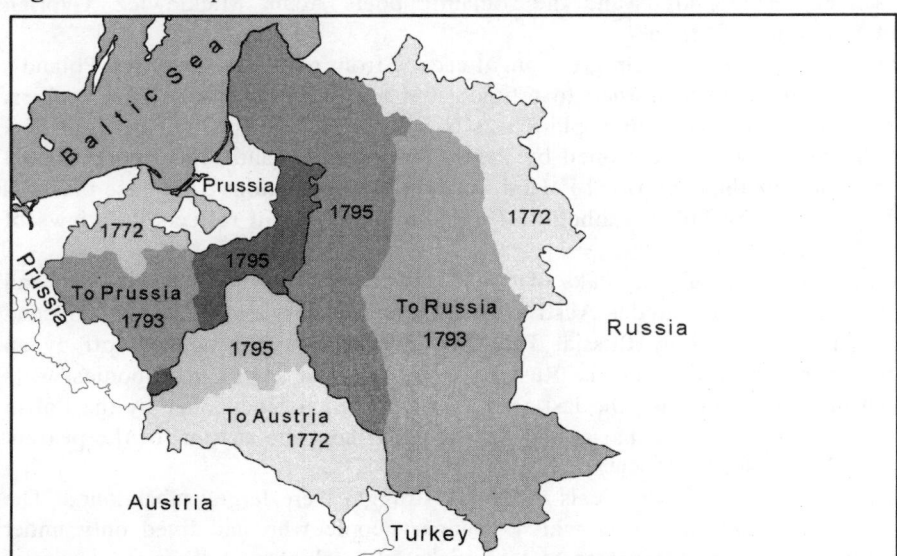

The Rebellions and the Great Migration

After the last partition, Poles became the subjects of three different kingdoms. For the bulk of the population, the peasants, little changed, at least in the initial stages. Their everyday life continued to be controlled by the same landowners, and the land had to be cultivated regardless of whose subjects they happened to be. The nobility, on the other hand, had much to lose. They therefore took to arms several times during the 70 years following the final partition in attempts to regain independence.

The first of these attempts was connected with Napoleon. A number of Polish nobles went to Italy, where they formed legions which fought alongside Napoleon's army. In 1806 this army entered former Polish territories, and in 1807 the Principality of Warsaw was established. However, after the final defeat and abdication of Napoleon, most of Poland was retaken by Austria, Prussia and Russia, except for the territory which the 1815 Congress of Vienna allocated to the Polish Kingdom.

The Polish Kingdom initially enjoyed some independence, including its own *Sejm* and army. This encouraged a conspiracy among the Polish nobles, which resulted in an armed insurrection against Russia in 1830–31. After the insurrection was quashed, the Polish Kingdom was fully incorporated into the Russian Empire and an intense campaign of national oppression and russification followed. Martial law was introduced, national universities were closed and the use of the Polish language in schools was prohibited. Similar restrictions were already in other parts of Poland which were under Austrian and German occupation.

After the failed insurrection, many of the Polish intellectuals fled the country. They settled mostly in France and southern Europe, where they played an important role in keeping the Polish national spirit alive. Included in the Great Migration were some of Poland's greatest thinkers, writers and composers, among them the famous composer Fryderyk Chopin and the romantic poets Adam Mickiewicz, Cyprian Norwid and Juliusz Słowacki.

Some of the prominent emigrés sought escape from reality by extolling Poland's past glories, while others turned to religion and mystic or messianic philosophies. The best known of these philosophies was based on the concept that the guilt of a corrupt humanity would be atoned by the sufferings of Poland. The romantic poet Adam Mickiewicz thus described Poland as 'the Christ of nations', a phrase that was picked up mainly by Polish Catholics. Today, this phrase still reflects the views of some Polish nationals.

Further unsuccessful outbreaks of armed resistance occurred between 1846 and 1848 in parts of Poland under Austrian and German rules, and between 1863 and 1864 in parts occupied by Russia. The 1863 insurrection was sparked off by an attempt to conscript Poles into the Russian army, and was one of the bloodiest wars in Polish history. It was also the last armed struggle for independence by the Polish nobility. Its failure showed that armed resistance without the support of the peasant masses could not succeed.

After 1864 the romantic ideals of armed struggle were largely abandoned. The age of reason followed, during which younger people who had lived only under occupation devoted their energies to 'organic work', which was designed to foster internal economic and social progress. As a result, industry, trade and agriculture were gradually modernised. The process was assisted by the opening up of the huge Russian Empire to trade with Poland. The country grew in strength and waited for the right time to reach out again for independence.

The Struggle for Independence

Shortly before the outbreak of World War I, Józef Piłsudski began to emerge as a potential leader in the struggle for independence. He began his political career as an active member of the terrorist wing of the Polish Socialist Party. When in 1906 he and other proponents of armed resistance were expelled from the party, Piłsudski established his own political camp, the aim of which was to train Polish military forces. He established links with Austrian military circles and set up Polish paramilitary organisations in parts of southern Poland which were occupied by Austria. Subsequently, at the 1912 Convention of Independence Activists—which was dominated by Piłsudski—the Polish Military Treasury was established to provide the necessary financial support for future Polish forces.

From the beginning of World War I the three powers that ruled Poland found themselves on opposite sides of the conflict and began to compete for the loyalty of their Polish subjects. Each promised that an independent Poland would be created at the end of the war. However, Piłsudski found that support offered by Austria for the August 1914 uprising in the Russian-occupied region of Kielce was only half-hearted. It was neither in Austria's nor in Germany's interest to foster a strong Polish force which they would have to reckon with later.

In 1917 Poles sided with the Allies after United States President Wilson declared that 'there should be a united, independent and autonomous Poland'. A Polish army was thus formed in France, which fought on the Western Front. At the same time, Piłsudski's First Brigade refused to swear allegiance to Germany, an action for which Piłsudski was imprisoned and was not released until the end of the war. At the end of the war, Piłsudski returned to Warsaw, where he became the Temporary Chief of State until 1922 when a constitution was adopted and new parliament was elected. The end of World War I on 11 November 1918 marks the re-emergence of Poland as an independent state.

The New Poland

The first task facing the new Polish state was to secure its borders. The Treaty of Versailles granted Poland most of the former Prussian territories—with a narrow corridor to the sea—and established Gdańsk as a free city. Disputed areas in the south (Silesia) were divided between Germany and Poland as a result of a plebiscite. The eastern border, on the other hand, almost immediately became a source of conflict between Poland and Soviet Russia. The conflict was finally settled with a peace treaty in 1921, when Bielorussia and the Ukraine were divided between Poland and

Russia. The last Polish borders were secured in 1922 when Polish forces took over the Lithuanian city of Vilnius and its surrounding regions.

The first few years of independent Poland were difficult. The political life of the country had to be reorganised, a constitution had to be written and free elections had to be held. This period of political instability ended in 1926 with a coup led by Józef Piłsudski. He seized power and held it until his death in 1935. A government made up of Piłsudski's close political and military associates was then formed and it remained in power until the outbreak of World War II.

Despite the initial political instability, the process of rebuilding the infrastructure and strength of the country began almost immediately after World War I. Agriculture, industry and commerce were developed and a number of ambitious projects were carried out. The best known of these was the construction of the entirely new port at Gdynia on the Baltic Sea. Poland had only a narrow corridor linking it to the Baltic Sea and Gdańsk was its only port. In 1924 the small fishing village of Gdynia was chosen as the site for a new port, and by 1939 it had been transformed into one of the largest and most modern ports on the Baltic.

The economic and the political developments in the new Poland were not destined to run their full course however. After Hitler came to power events in Germany gained momentum, culminating in the Anschluss with Austria, annexation of Czechoslovakia and on 1 September 1939 an attack on Poland. Two weeks later, on 17 September 1939, Soviet Union also attacked Poland and occupied the eastern territories regained by Poland in 1921. This was the start of World War II.

World War II

The Nazi atrocities committed in occupied Poland have been well documented and described in numerous publications. Some 6 million Polish citizens died during World War II. About half of these were Jews, most of whom were methodically killed in concentration camps set up by the Nazis. Many of the 3 million ethnic Poles died in Nazi concentration camps, but almost as many were either executed after the Russian invasion in 1939—one well known example being the killing of some 15 000 Polish officers by Soviet NKVD, of whom about 4000 are known to have been murdered in the Katyn Forest—or perished after they were 'resettled' in Siberia between 1939 and 1942. Also, hundreds of thousands died as members of the Home Army, fighting on Polish soil or on various battlefields of the war. Among these were the Polish pilots, who played a significant role in the Battle of Britain, and Polish armed forces who took part in the battle of France in 1940, in the 1941-43 African Campaign and on the Western and Eastern fronts in 1944 and 1945.

The liberation of Poland in 1945 came from the east. At the end of July 1944 the Russian Red Army approached Warsaw and stopped on the banks of the Vistula River. In a desperate attempt to seize the control of the capital and establish a constitutional government, the Polish resistance movement (the pro-Western Home Army) staged a bloody uprising against the occupying Nazis. The Russian army, realising that the resistance movement would be a force to reckon with in post-war

Poland, simply stood on the other side of the Vistula and watched as some 200 000 resistance fighters perished in a two month long struggle. The Soviets even refused landing rights to Allied planes which carried weapons and ammunition for the Home Army. When the Red Army finally entered Warsaw on 17 January 1945 it was a city from which most of the population had been deported and in which buildings had been methodically destroyed by German demolition teams. This was a perfect setting for establishing a Soviet-backed government without any significant resistance from the local population.

Poland's fate was sealed at the Yalta Conference in February 1945. Most Poles consider that the Western Allies gave in to Soviet demands on all fronts. As a result, Poland's pre-war eastern borders were moved west to what is known as the Curzon Line and the western border was moved to the Odra and Nysa rivers. Furthermore, the Allies agreed to recognise a Soviet-backed government and to no longer recognise Poland's London-based Government in Exile. There was, however, a proviso in the agreement that democratic elections would be held in Poland at a later date.

Post-War Poland

After twenty years of independence and six years of German occupation, Poland was again ruled by Russian-backed government. The Communist Government was installed in Warsaw in 1945 and immediately began ruthless elimination of potential anti-communist resistance. When the elections were finally held in 1947, they were marred by intimidation and vote rigging, which ensured that the Communists stayed in power. For the next four decades the Communist Party ruled Poland, while the Polish Government in Exile continued to exist in London.

Inside Poland, the remaining remnants of the Home Army and other pro-Western military units organised themselves in remote forests and offered armed resistance. This was crushed within three years of the Communist takeover, but the resistance did not cease—only its form changed. In 1956 in Poznań, Communist Party buildings were burned during demonstrations, which led to the removal of hardline Stalinists from the Government. In 1968 anti-communist student demonstrations were held at all universities, followed in 1970 by industrial strikes in the port cities and in Silesia, and in 1975 in Central Poland. Towards the end of the 1970s, all opposition movements joined to form the Solidarity movement, which became prominent during the nationwide strikes of August 1980. The Government relented to the strikers' demands and Solidarity was officially registered. It thus became the first independent trade union in the Communist Block.

Legalisation of Solidarity marked the beginning of the end of Communist rule not only in Poland but also in other communist countries of Eastern Europe. The Communist Party had stayed in power for over 40 years mainly because of the military and political support from the Soviet Union. Dissatisfaction among the people was ever-present, however, particularly because there were insufficient improvements in the country's economy and in the standard of living of the industrial workers who were meant to benefit the most under communism. The pressure for

Figure 2.4   Polish borders in 1922 and 1945.

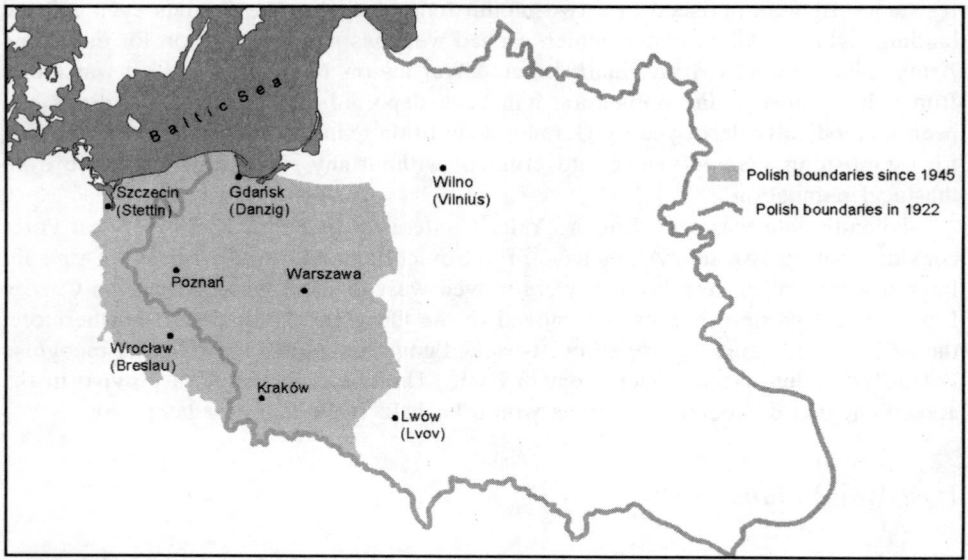

change grew until in 1989 a new, non-communist government took over, the first in Eastern Europe. Free presidential elections were held in 1990 and the Government in Exile could be finally disbanded. Poland had at last regained full independence.

Polish history is clearly unique, characterised by a long struggle for independence. It is not surprising then that Poles take a keen interest in their history and are proud of their country's achievements, which have helped them maintain their national identity and hope despite many setbacks. Poles tend to be strongly nationalistic, aware of the role Poland's powerful neighbours have played in frustrating its efforts to be independent. This nationalism has anti-German, anti-Russian and, particularly, anti-communist overtones. Also, Poland's past experiences causes many Poles to question whether the changes taking place at present in Eastern Europe are permanent or simply another brief episode in history.

Polish Society

Since the abolition of the Communist Government in 1989, Polish society has been going through the process of changing its political, economic and social structures. This process may take a whole generation to complete. To understand the present society, therefore, it is important to first examine the country's past and then its future, because the attitudes, values and living conditions of most Poles today are largely the result of the last 200 years of Poland's history and, in particular, of 45 years of Communist rule.

The Communist Government did not gain the support of the majority of the population, and opposition to it did not cease even during the 10 years of strict

Stalinist rule, during which the activities of resistance groups were severely punished. Moreover, there was a lot of dissatisfaction because it soon became apparent that average working class Poles were worse off economically under the Communists than they had been before. Even though the policy of full employment guaranteed jobs for everyone, salaries were low and, consequently, family incomes were barely above the subsistence level.

In 1956, after worker strikes in Poznań, Władysław Gomułka took over as the new Communist Party leader and promised to take the country on a 'Polish road to socialism', without collectivisation of agriculture and with some allowances for small private enterprises. A short period of calm followed, but little changed. At the beginning of the 1960s political opposition among the intellectuals reappeared, resulting in a wave of demonstrations and student strikes in 1968. At the same time, working class people were becoming increasingly dissatisfied with their poor living conditions, bringing about a wave of strikes in the coastal cities in 1970. The 1970s saw more strikes and a gradual unification of various opposition groups. This led to the formation of the Solidarity movement, which was the main force behind the collapse of Poland's Communist Government in 1989.

When examining Polish contemporary society it is important to remember that the majority of Poles have spent most of their lives in opposition to their government, living in a country in which the economy was almost totally state owned. As a result, Poles tend to have certain negative attitudes which are not often held by people in developed democratic countries. These include an attitude of defiance toward the government and senior management. Until recently, people in authority were scorn-fully labelled as *oni* (they), as opposed to *my* (us)—that is, the rest of the nation. There was a general lack of enthusiasm for the low-paid work in state enterprises and office work was characterised by the saying: *Czy się stoi, czy się leży, dwa tysiące się należy* (Whether you work or while away, 2000 [zloty] will always come your way). There was also a general acceptance of dishonest practices such as cheating the employer by working shorter hours, slowing down the production and taking goods for private use from state enterprise stocks. It was acceptable to use usefully placed friends and relations, and to use bribes to achieve goals.

Opposition to authority and difficult conditions have, on the other hand, devel-oped strong interpersonal ties and a strong feeling of solidarity among ordinary Poles, even among strangers. The fact that the Communist Government was backed by former Soviet Union has meant that there were among Poles anti-Russian feelings as well as opposition to communism. The attitudes towards the West, however, were quite different. The Iron Curtain prevented most Poles from travelling outside the Eastern Block, their direct contact with the West being therefore often limited to letters, parcels and money sent by their immigrant relatives. This contributed to misconceptions about life in the West.

Since the change of government in 1989, negative attitudes towards the author-ities have begun to slowly change. However, the introduction of Western style of economy—into a country that is debt ridden, burdened by inefficient enterprises and whose workforce is not used to efficient production—will take longer to bring about positive results. Many Poles are only now beginning to realise that life in a capitalist democratic society is not necessarily easy.

The strong nationalistic feelings remain mainly because united Germany in the west and Russia—despite the collapse of the Soviet Union—in the east still loom as potential threats to Poland's security. Mixed with the nationalistic feelings is the religious fervour. Under the Communist Government the activities of the Catholic Church were strongly discouraged in the Government's attempts to secularise the society, but since the change of government in 1989, the Church has experienced great revival.

The Catholic Church

When Mieszko I was baptised into the Catholic Church in 966, no-one could have predicted that the word 'Polish' would be almost synonymous with Catholicism. The position of the Catholic Church in Poland in the 10th century was not different to that in other European countries. When the Reformation swept Europe in the 16th century, the Catholic Church in Poland was not affected permanently, but, at the same time, the Polish-Lithuanian Commonwealth had within its borders the Orthodox Church and its sect, the Uniats, a substantial Jewish population and a number of Protestant groups who had fled from less tolerant countries.

The position of the Catholic Church changed at the end of the 18th century after Poland's neighbours began occupying parts of Poland on the pretext of protecting the rights of the non-Catholic minorities. Since the majority of Russians in Poland were Orthodox and most of the Prussians were Protestant, the Catholic Church came to be associated with the ethnic Poles. This association was strengthened during the 19th century when the country was ruled by three different administrations and the Catholic Church was the only institution which existed legally in all parts of Poland. Consequently, it played a role in maintaining the Polish linguistic and cultural identity and in armed insurrections against the partitioning powers. Catholic clergy not only offered shelter to resistance fighters, but many went into battle themselves.

At the end of World War II Poland lost its eastern provinces, together with most of its non-Catholic population. The communist system, which openly declared its hostility to religion, was thus introduced into a country that was relatively homogenous, both as far as its religion was concerned and ethnically. It is not surprising then that the majority of Poles who were opposed to the new system joined the Church—which was threatened by communism—in opposition to the Government. At the time when churches in Western Europe were going through a period of decline, the Catholic Church in Poland grew, with many Poles turning to their priests for consolation and spiritual leadership. During the Stalinist period, when it was dangerous to show open opposition to the Government, attendance at Sunday mass provided a relatively safe opportunity to demonstrate defiance of the authorities.

Even though relations between the Government and the Church improved after the removal of the hardline Stalinists from the Government in 1956 and a number of leftist Christian politicians were able to contest seats in the *Sejm* (Polish Parliament), the Church continued to support dissident groups. This support increased during the 1970s when the Church, together with lay opposition organisations, provided moral and material assistance to the families of workers who were killed or imprisoned as a result of the strikes.

The greatest boost the opposition movements and Poles as a whole received was when in 1978 a Polish cardinal, Karol Wojtyła, was elected Pope (John Paul II) and soon after visited Poland. Hundreds of thousands attended the public masses celebrated by the Pope and millions watched the event on television. It was then that Poles realised that they had the numbers to overthrow the Communist regime. The 1980 nationwide strikes and the creation of Solidarity followed soon after.

The Catholic Church played an extremely important role during the final years of Communist rule in Poland. After the introduction of martial law in December 1981, churches became hiding places for those opposing the regime, venues for secret meetings and for performances of banned theatrical works. Sunday sermons were almost the only source of uncensored information. Consequently, the Church played a vital role in the negotiations between Solidarity and the Government in 1989, which resulted in the final collapse of the Communist regime.

Now that Poland has a freely elected parliament and government, the Church's role as a supporter of opposition is over. However, it has not ceased to be politically active. The Church still exerts considerable influence in the Polish Parliament through Christian political parties such as the Christian Democrats. Christian politicians are actively pushing the Church's line on such contentious issues as abortion and the reintroduction of religion into schools. Thus, in Poland, religion continues to play an important part in Poles' private as well as their public life.

Polish Nationalism

The term 'nationalism' as it is used here refers to the feelings and attitudes that most Polish nationals share towards their country, their culture and towards other Poles, as well as towards other ethnic groups and nationalities. Poles living in Poland, as well as Polish immigrants abroad, are well known for their very strong sense of national identity. These strong nationalistic feelings are the result of the country's turbulent history. It must be pointed out, however, that the attitudes of the younger generations who have been brought up in post-war Poland differ somewhat from those of the older Poles.

Nationalistic feelings can be manifested either in positive or in negative ways. In case of Poles living in Poland, these feelings have helped to maintain a sense of national identity and to unite the Poles in their struggles for independence. Nationalism is now helping to maintain social stability during the difficult time of change.

A detailed discussion of issues relating to Polish nationalism is beyond the scope of this book, thus only two aspects of Polish nationalism will be looked at here. These are the attitudes Poles have towards their neighbours and the Jews, and their sensitivity towards themselves and their heritage. These two aspects of Polish nationalism strongly influence the way Poles view other people and adapt to life in other countries.

Poles are sometimes accused of harbouring negative attitudes towards almost all of their neighbouring nations and towards the Jews. This, however, is an oversimplification of the actual situation. While elements of anti-German, anti-Russian and anti-Jewish sentiment can certainly be found among Poles, they are by no means shared by all Polish people. Furthermore, the intensity of these feelings has changed over time according to political and social situations.

Poles' Attitudes Towards Germany

Poland has had to cope with military threats along its western border from the very beginning of its existence. In fact, the main reason why Mieszko I adopted Christianity was to prevent the Germans from introducing it by force. During most of Poland's history Germany has either engaged in war with Poland or occupied parts of its territory. Despite this, the relationship between the two countries has not been entirely a negative one.

Germany was a well established country when Poland came into existence and it had much to offer to the new member of the Christian family of nations, including trade. A number of German institutions served as models for similar Polish establishments, some of German laws were either used in their original form or adapted to Polish conditions and, except in time of war, there was a steady stream of German immigrants settling in the new towns and on uninhabited land. Generally, anti-German feelings were prevalent during wartime, but they tended to be much less present in times of peace.

The 20th century is typical in that respect. The two world wars fuelled anti-German sentiment, which was felt most intensely during World War II. This feeling, however, is no longer shared by the younger, post-war generation. In fact, there is every indication that, having secured associate membership of the European Community in 1991, Poland is on the verge of a long period of peaceful and friendly coexistence with Germany.

Poles' Attitudes Towards Russia

Poland's relationship with its eastern neighbours is very different to that with Germany. Initially, Polish rulers pursued a similar policy towards the Lithuanians, Ukrainians and the Russians as the Germans did towards Poland, in that they conquered as much land to the east as they could. Towards the end of the 14th century this resulted in the union with Lithuania, which made the Polish-Lithuanian Commonwealth a strong power in Europe. However, at about the same time, the Duchy of Muscovy began to expand rapidly and soon became Poland's most dangerous threat.

Today, after 130 years of Russian occupation and almost 50 years of a Soviet-backed Communist Government, Poles are still very weary of Russia. They may find it difficult to agree about any other political or ethnic issue, but they all have the same deep suspicion of Russia.

Poles' Attitudes Towards Jews

Unlike Poles' attitudes towards the Germans and the Russians, the Polish-Jewish question is mainly an internal matter. It has been complicated by the fact that during the last 200 years Poles and Jews have developed a love-hate relationship.

Jews began arriving in Poland during the reign of the Piast Dynasty, well before Poland was founded in 966. Their numbers increased steadily, and until the partitions at the end of 18th century, they enjoyed rights and privileges as one of the fully recognised peoples within the Polish society. As a result, four-fifths of world Jewry at the time of the partitions lived within the boundaries of the Polish-Lithuanian Commonwealth.

After Poland was partitioned, however, the relationship between the Jews and the Poles changed. As Davis (1985) points out:

> . . . a measure of intercommunal animosity was perhaps inevitable. It was encouraged by the age-old social and economic deformations of Polish and Jewish society, by poverty and demographic pressures, and above all, by the growing tendency in Eastern Europe for all national groups to seek their own separate salvation in their own separate way. Polish hostility towards the Jews was complemented by Jewish hostility towards the Poles. In an age of rampant nationalism, intercommunal solidarity was badly hampered. So long as the Empires of the partitioning powers remained in place, the numerous renascent nations of the region were trapped like rats in a cage, where it was easier to bite one's neighbour than to break down the bars of the common servitude. (p. 258)

Unfortunately, the course of history in the 20th century encouraged extremist elements in both groups to continue accusing each other. Despite attempts at reconciliation undertaken by more moderate forces in independent Poland between the wars and after the overthrow of the Communist Government, a degree of animosity between Poles and Jews persists. This has not however prevented ordinary Poles and Jews from developing personal friendships, intermarrying, being partners in business, sharing pleasure and sorrow, and contributing significantly to both cultures.

Poles' Attitudes Towards Themselves

The most striking characteristic of Poles living abroad is their pride in being Polish. They show this in various ways. If, for instance, a Polish person is introduced without their origins being mentioned, they will soon point that out in the conversation, regardless of whether it is asked for or not. The reason for this can be illustrated by what Dorothy, a Polish immigrant, said soon after she received her Australian citizenship. After she had asserted in a conversation that she was Polish, she was asked why she needed to do that. Her reply was: 'I want people to know that I am

Polish, to recognise me for what I am.' In other words, Dorothy was not saying that she lacked commitment to Australia, only that she was unwilling to deny her roots.

Because of Poland's troubled history, and especially because of the partition of Poland, the distinction between citizenship and nationality has assumed great significance to Poles. Many Polish immigrants believe they did not leave Poland by choice, and they have hence developed the urge to assert their Polish identity.

Most Poles also like to speak well of their country's history and culture, and are very sensitive to any criticism of it. However, due to the fact that Poland's achievements in the last 200 years have been limited, any discussion of them is difficult. Consequently, many Poles, especially older people, tend to dwell on the grandeur of Poland's distant past and have a tendency to overestimate the role Poland has played during the last 200 years. They sometimes even attribute to it a role of messianic proportions.

It is not surprising then that negative statements about Poland's history, lack of awareness that Poland existed as a state for many centuries or ignorance of its geographical location may be considered by many Poles to be extremely offensive, especially if Poles are confused with their neighbours, particularly the Russians. Typically, Polish immigrants react by pointing out that their country of adoption has had a comparatively short history, and they then follow this with a negative comment on the subject.

While there is no doubt that the overall achievements of Poland's Communist Government were not impressive, it cannot be denied that during the 50 year rule Poles had access to inexpensive books and cinemas, there was state sponsorship for the arts and museums and free education was guaranteed for all. Most people in Poland could not accumulate material wealth, but they did acquire at least high school education and many went on to university studies. Rather than wealth, education helped people to move up the social ladder because the intelligentsia were held in high regard. Consequently, today's younger generation is well educated and proud of that fact. Most of them see Polish culture as part of the broader stream of Western European civilisation, to which they feel they belong.

It follows then that while both the younger and the older generations of Poles share strong ties with their homeland, the majority of the post-war generation are more pragmatic and culture oriented than the older generation, less inclined to mysticism and symbolic gestures and, generally speaking, relate better to foreigners. The case of Anna, a 30 year old Polish immigrant to Australia, serves as a good example. Anna is a student and during a class in linguistics her tutor illustrated a point by quoting a phrase, which used by a Polish immigrant in a pub did not include the word 'please'. Anna would not have taken any special note of what the tutor was saying but then the tutor, who knew Anna was Polish, made the mistake of interrupting the lecture and asking her whether it was normal for Polish people not to use the word 'please'. Anna, who was somewhat agitated by this, thought for a moment and then explained to her tutor politely that the Polish immigrant could have had a language problem since the word 'please' was used in Polish as often as in English and that, in any case, the bar was not the best place to look for polite language usage by immigrants or by true-blue Aussies. Anna belongs to the younger generation of Poles, but if she was from the older generation, she would have probably become aggressive, or she might have even walked out of the class following the tutor's question.

In summary, it must be said that Poles, who can be extremely critical of almost every aspect of life in Poland when in the company of other Poles, tend to become intolerant of such criticism by foreigners. In this they are not different from some other ethnic groups who have settled in English speaking countries such as Australia, Canada and the United States.

The Promised Land of Capitalism

Before 1989, most Poles did not travel outside the Eastern Block. Even today, after the Iron Curtain has been brought down, many Poles have never been outside Poland. For many Poles, the image of the West is based on what they had seen in films, contact they have with relatives who have emigrated, stories told by those who had an opportunity to go to Western countries for brief visits and from observation of the behaviour of Westerners who visit Poland. Consequently, most Poles have a false image of what life is like in a capitalist society.

Until recently, government subsidies made food and manufactured goods relatively cheap in Poland. The latter were hard to get, however, and often of poor quality. Consequently, the value of hard currency, which could be used to buy good quality Western goods, was blown out of all proportion by the black market. The average monthly salary, for example, was worth on the black market $US50, yet its purchasing power for locally produced goods was sufficient for an average family to maintain a life style similar to that of Western families living on unemployment benefit. In other words, the purchasing power of the average salary was actually much higher than it was in hard currency.

The Western world seemed to most Poles to be a place where people did not have to work too hard to be rich and have fun. This 'Hollywood' image was reinforced by their relatives in the West who usually wrote about the positive aspects of their experience and sent photographs of their lovely homes and leisure activities. Their earnings, when calculated in Polish zlotys at black market prices, seemed astronomical. Also the spending power of tourists and relatives visiting Poland seemed very impressive. Even when Poles went for short periods of time to Western countries to earn hard currency, they did not get the chance to fully comprehend the reality of life in the West because they did not pay taxes or have regular expenses. In most cases, their accommodation and daily needs were provided by friends or relatives with whom they were staying. Everything they earned was saved to be spent in Poland, where the value of hard currencies was excessively high.

It was not surprising then that all efforts by communist propaganda to depict life in the West in negative terms did not succeed. Such propaganda was not believed as a matter of principle and, besides, the facts as they were perceived from inside Poland suggested the opposite. The West seemed like a promised land, where work was abundant, salaries were very high and success was guaranteed as long as permanent residence in a Western country could be secured.

The most apparent effect of this misconception was several big waves of refugees who sought political asylum in the West. Each wave followed a period of political upheaval, which usually brought about a brief period of relaxation of passport restrictions. However, this was soon followed by restoration of full government control and persecution. Some emigrants in the 1956, 1968, 1970 and 1981 waves were genuine refugees, but the majority left for purely economic reasons. Unfortunately, many immigrants were ill prepared for life in the West. They had very high expectations and were shocked when they realised that it would take them many years of hard work to reach the material goals they had set for themselves, and that success was by no means guaranteed.

This false image of the West had, on the other hand, a positive effect on the struggle against the Communist regime in Poland. From the early 1960s onwards, strikes and demonstrations were accompanied not only by political, anti-communist slogans, but also by an ever-growing demand for a change from a state-run to a capitalist economy. It was, in fact, the false image of a capitalist society that made many Poles believe that the collapse of the Communist Government would lead to economic changes almost overnight. As a result, many of those who actually fought against communism and contributed to the present state of affairs, are now undergoing a 'cultural shock' inside their own country, which has failed to live up to their unrealistic expectations. In particular, the elderly, who have to live on low pensions, and people in their 40s and 50s, who find it hard to adjust to the new conditions—often seeing themselves as the 'lost generation'—have found the experience most difficult. They have spent half of their working lives in a state-run economy and now find it hard to give up their old habit of blaming the authorities for everything, including personal failure.

The driving forces behind the dramatic changes taking place in Poland today are a group of dynamic business people and people in their 20s and 30s. They are bringing about reform at a very rapid pace, which was evident to the author when he visited the country in 1990 and in 1993. In 1990 Poland was a rather disorganised country, where loopholes in the system were used to make shady deals, crime was on the rise and most average Poles still worked in state enterprises. The two most striking features of Poland in 1990 were thousands of small traders who were selling goods from camp beds put up on pavements, and an overwhelming attitude of resignation among middle-aged people. The Poland that the author saw in 1993, however, was a country on the move. Today, there is a thriving stock exchange in Warsaw and international business deals are being made daily. In the big cities, street traders have moved to specially designed bazaars or to regular shops, all of which are well stocked and full of customers. Many of those who initially had difficulties are beginning to adjust and have found better jobs and some hope.

The negative side of this growth has been the closure of thousands of state enterprises, which has created a huge unemployment problem. This is especially so in smaller towns, in which there was usually only one large factory where most of the workforce was employed. After the closures, people who did not establish their own businesses or did not find new jobs became dependent on the unemployment benefit or a pension, and became poorer than ever. Thus, if one goes to the outer suburbs of big cities or to smaller towns, one can see that there is the same hopeless struggle for survival. The difference is that now, because in some areas there is wealth, this struggle for survival is more painful to bear than before. It is the people who find themselves in such situations who tend to have an idealised view of the West. It is they who are the most likely candidates for emigration during the next decade. If they do emigrate, they may find more of their hopes dashed.

---

1. Andrzej Walicki claims that:

> Poland is a country where everything has a historical dimension. We are living, as it were, with the entire burden of our history on our shoulders, without being able to forget about the past, or to liberate ourselves from its omnipresent influence. (Walicki 1990, p. 21.)

(a) To what extent do you think the history of your country influences contemporary attitudes?

(b) What aspects of that history most influence contemporary attitudes?

2. What criticisms do foreigners most often make about Poland?

3. To what extent do you think these criticisms are justified?

4. How do you feel when you hear such criticism?

CHAPTER THREE

POLISH AND ENGLISH LANGUAGES COMPARED

There is a strong connection between language and culture, in the sense that language shapes as well as reflects the social and cultural aspects of a given language community. Thus, the English language has shaped and now reflects elements of various cultures in English speaking countries, as does the Polish language in regard to Polish culture.

Polish is a western Slavonic language. It includes a number of dialects which used to be spoken within the historical boundaries of Poland. These dialects came to be used less over time as the gradual codification of written and spoken Polish, the increasing availability of education and the influence of the mass media encouraged the use of standardised Polish. The dialects are still used in some regions, but the official language throughout Poland today is standard Polish.

Polish belongs to the Indo-European family of languages. This group of languages was in turn split into several groups which over time developed independently. One of these was the Germanic group which included English, and another was the Slavonic group which included Polish.

Although Polish is a Slavonic language, it shares many features with Romance and Germanic languages because of the cultural and linguistic influences from Western Europe. When Catholicism was introduced into Poland in the 10th century, Latin was adopted as the language of the Church and learning. It continued to be used as such until the middle of the 18th century. In the 16th century, Bona Sforza, the Italian wife of King Sigismunt I, introduced into Poland the Italian culture, including its architecture, art and cuisine, which has influenced certain usages in the language over the centuries. During the 17th and 18th centuries, French language and culture became fashionable among the educated classes, while German language continued to be used in the cities and some country areas where many German burghers and farmers lived. The German influence increased considerably after the partitions at the end of the 18th century.

Due to these outside influences, the Polish and English languages have much in common, particularly the influences of Latin and French. It is not surprising then that while Polish and English differ significantly in some respects, there are many similarities between them, especially in vocabulary.

The similarities between the two languages can be of a considerable help in the English language classroom, but it is important to remember that there are also some very important differences. Some are simply differences of form, while others concern relationships between form and cultural patterns—which will be dealt with later—and may be much more difficult to tackle.

Sounds and Spelling

Most of the vowels and consonants used in Polish are roughly similar to those used in English. Nevertheless, Poles learning English tend to have problems with pronunciation. First, they have problems with pronunciation because in certain instances the Polish language uses fewer sounds than English. For example, Polish uses two vowels—[a] and [e]—whereas English uses five—[aː], [a], [æ], [∂] and [e]. Second, Polish uses more sounds than English because it has the palatalised [s] and the alveolar [š], whereas English has just one sound, [ʃ]. Third, some sounds are used in one language but not in the other. English uses sounds such as [θ] and [đ], which are not used in the Polish phonological system, while Polish has nasal [ą] and [ę], which do not exist in English. Unlike some other Slavonic languages however, Polish has a very easy set of rules governing stress, which always falls on the second-to-last syllable of the word.

Polish uses the Latin alphabet, with the addition of several diacritical marks. Because there are more sounds to be represented than available letters in the alphabet, Polish also includes a few two-letter combinations to denote one sound. Generally speaking, Polish spelling is much simpler than English, for it is a system in which a given letter, or combination of letters, always represents the same sound. The fact that there are several devoicing and voicing rules does not make the system much more difficult, since these rules have few exceptions and once learned can be

Table 3.1 Pronunciation of Polish letters.

Polish	Nearest English equivalent	Polish	Nearest English equivalent
a	hut	l	lamp
ą	song	ł	win
b	big	m	mine
c	hits	n	nice
ć	cheat	ń	niece
ch	hat	o	pot
cz	child	ó	look
d	do	p	spin
dz	lads	r	rude (trilled
dż	jet	rz	leisure
dź	Jean	s	sit
e	let	ś	sheep
ę	length	sz	sure
f	fit	t	step
g	get	u	look
h	hat	w	very
i	beat	y	very
j	yes	z	zoo
k	skin	ź	measure
		ż	measure

followed easily. Table 3.1 on the previous page is a rough guide to the pronunciation of Polish letters, which should help those who do not speak Polish to at least correctly pronounce Polish names.

Vocabulary

There are several similarities between Polish and English vocabularies, many of which can be attributed to similar cultural developments. The vocabulary used by both languages in the humanities and sciences is based on Latin and Greek both include German-based words and both languages have borrowed from French vocabulary the words they use in the arts and diplomacy. For example, an English person needs no knowledge of Polish to recognise such words as *student, uniwersytet, klasa, bakteria, biologia, chemia, plastyk, aktor, teatr, literatura, architekt, prezydent, kil* and *minister*. Even though some of these words have a slightly different spelling, a different ending or a different pronunciation, they are easily recognised.

English and Polish also have many words which have precisely the same meaning in both languages, but which are different in form. For example, the Polish words *grzech, zło, dobro, księżyc, wiatr, przeszłość* and *zwycięstwo* have exactly the same connotations as the English words sin, evil, goodness, moon, wind, past and victory respectively. This is mainly because both languages are part of the same Western European culture, a fact that has influenced the way Poles and English speakers perceive the world around them.

There are also significant differences in the vocabularies of the two languages. One of these is the availability or lack of words in certain areas. For example, maritime and weather terminology is much better developed in English than in Polish. This is because Britain has had close connection with the sea throughout its history, whereas Poland to this day has very limited access to the coast. Polish has, therefore, borrowed much of its maritime and weather terminology from Dutch, English and German languages. English also uses a number of words which are to do with these two subject areas but which do not have exact Polish equivalents. Other areas in which exact equivalents do not exist are words denoting various phenomena—for example, Christmas Eve denotes in Polish a holy day, whereas in Australia it is the last day to shop for presents—institutions and activities which are specific to a given country. Here the differences between Polish and American, Australian, British and Canadian English are significant.

Idioms, sayings and fixed phrases also tend to differ, since they are usually related more to a country's cultural patterns than to developments within the Indo-European family of languages. For instance, the meaning of phrases such as 'true-blue [Aussie]', or 'fair dinkum' would be very hard to translate, since neither of these concepts correspond exactly to anything in Polish.

Grammar

Polish and English languages differ the most in their grammars, even though some of their word derivations are similar. Polish is basically an inflected language—that is, it depends heavily on inflected word endings to denote their function—with fewer restrictions on word order than English. Also unlike English, it includes grammatical gender, seven grammatical cases and certain categories of verbs which are specific to it. There are also considerable differences in the syntax.

Word Derivations

Word derivations in Polish and English show some similarities and some differences, as illustrated in Table 3.2 below. As in English, in Polish the linguistic rules which govern morphemes (word stems, prefixes and suffixes) allow nouns and adjectives to be derived from verbs, adverbs and nouns from adjectives, and adjectives and verbs from nouns. While morphemes themselves are mostly language specific, the way in which families of words are created by joining them or by adding prefixes and suffixes are often similar. For example, in both languages adverbs are often derived from adjectives by adding a specific suffix to the stem—'-ly' in English and '-o' or '-e' in Polish—as shown in Table 3.2 below.

A good example of differences are Polish diminutives which are more numerous and more frequently used than are diminutives in English. For instance, English has three forms of 'mother': mother, mum and mummy—the last one is used mainly by small children. Polish, on the other hand, has at least nine: *matka, mama, mamusia, mamuśka, mateczka, mateńka, matusieńka, matuś, mamula*—all of which are used by children and adults alike to address their mothers.

Polish Inflectional System

Polish is an inflected language which uses inflected word endings to indicate the functions of nouns, adjectives, pronouns, numerals and verbs. English, on the other hand, has shed most of its inflectional endings and now uses only a few inflections to distinguish singular and plural nouns and certain forms of the verb.

In Polish there are three types of word endings used to denote feminine, neuter and masculine genders. These are used at the end of nouns, adjectives, pronouns and numerals, and as gender indicators in some verb forms. Polish has seven grammatical cases of nouns, adjectives, pronouns and numerals, each with different suffixes for singular and plural forms. Likewise, the person of the verb whether first, second or

Table 3.2 Examples of adverbs derived from adjectives by addition of suffixes.

	Adjectives	Adverbs
English	quick	quick+ly
	nice	nice+ly
Polish	szybk+i	szybk+o
	przyjemn+y	przyjemni+e

third), the gender of the subject it refers to and, to a large extent, its tense are denoted by inflectional means. For example, the English noun 'book' can have only two endings, depending on whether it is used in the singular (book + 0) or the plural (book + s). Both forms can be used as subject and direct or indirect object, and both can form part of a prepositional phrase. In Polish, the equivalent word *książka* has seven singular endings (*książk + a, książk + i, książk + ę, książk + e, książk + ą, książk + e* and *książk +o*) as well as seven plural endings. These endings denote the specific syntactic function of the word. For example, the nominative case ending –*a* of *ksiazka* indicates the grammatical gender of the word (feminine in this case) and the fact that it is the subject. When it is the object, the genitive case ending –*i* is used, and when it is the indirect object, the dative case ending –*e* is used.

Verbs

The use of verbs is one of the aspects of English Polish learners find most difficult, mainly because of the different way tense and aspect are expressed in the two languages. In English, it is necessary first to decide whether a verb is in the past, present or future tense. It is then possible to indicate that the action is completed by using the perfect form, or that it is in progress by using the progressive form. In Polish, on the other hand, aspect is expressed by first making a choice between a perfective or an imperfective verb and then by using it in the past, present or future tense. Thus, for example, the Polish sentence:

> *Jan czyta Biblię.*

which uses the verb *czyta* (to read) in the present tense, could have at least three English translations, each conveying a slightly different message about an on-going activity. These are:

> John is reading the Bible.
> John reads the Bible.
> John has been reading the Bible.

Neither the Polish sentence nor the three English translations suggest that John has actually completed reading the Bible. To indicate that in English, the present perfect tense of the same verb 'to read' would be used. In Polish—which does not have perfect tenses—a perfective verb would be used instead. Thus the perfective verb *przeczytać* (denoting a completed action) would be used in the past tense, as follows:

> *Jan przeczytał Biblię.*
> (John has read the Bible.)

Because of these different uses of tenses, Poles tend to use the simple past tense when in English they should use the past perfect tense, and they tend to use either the simple past or the present tense when they should use the present perfect tense. Often the future perfect tense is incomprehensible to most Polish learners of English.

Another characteristic difference between the two verb systems is that in Polish the inflected ending of a verb indicates the person whom the verb is referring to. In English this is used only in the third person singular of the simple present tense (for example, 'He sits.'). Even then, unless a proper noun is used, a pronoun has to be included to specify the subject of the sentence. Polish, on the other hand, marks all finite verb forms for persons, as can be seen in the present tense singular of the verb *czytać* (to read):

> *czyta + m*
> *czyta + sz*
> *czyta + 0*

In this verb each person has a different ending. The same is true of all conjugations of tenses.

The other major differences between Polish and English are: Polish has only two ways of expressing the conditional mood while English has three; the passive voice is used much less frequently in Polish than in English which uses the imperative more frequently; and there is no strict sequence of tenses in Polish.

Definite and Indefinite Articles

Polish does not use definite and indefinite articles, the use of which Slavs learning English find particularly difficult to learn. The difficulty seems to be partly due to a lack of proper learner-oriented explanations and clear definitions of the problem. Many Poles who may be fluent in English still continue to occasionally use the articles incorrectly.

Syntax

English depends largely on word order, prepositions and pronouns to denote such syntactic functions as subject, direct and indirect objects and complements, as well as relationships between subject and predicate. Polish, on the other hand, uses gender, number and case endings to denote syntactic functions of nouns, adjectives, pronouns and numerals. Inflections are also used to denote the verb's person and gender. Within each sentence, the number, case and gender of nouns and their complements, as well as those of subjects and predicates, have to be in agreement.

Consequently, in Polish word order is much more flexible than in English, and pronouns are used less frequently. For example, in the sentence:

> John killed Mary.

John is the subject and Mary is the object. If the positions of the two proper nouns were changed, the sentence would read:

> Mary killed John.

The meaning of the sentence would change because in English the position of the noun in relation to the verb determines whether it is the subject or the object of the sentence. In Polish, it is the grammatical case of the noun that determines whether the noun is the subject or the object of the sentence. The subject of the sentence will always appear in the nominative case and the direct object in either the genitive or the accusative case. Thus, if the first of the above sentences was translated into Polish without changing the word order, it would read:

Jan zabił Marysię.

The noun *Jan* has nominative case ending and *Marysię* has the ending *–ę*, which means that it is in the accusative case. If the positions of the nouns are changed without the case endings being altered, the sentence would read:

Marysię zabił Jan.

Marysia is still the object of Jan's action and the change in the word order has only had a slight effect on the emphasis of the message.

Poles learning English will often be careless about the word order or they will use word order that is permissible in Polish but not in English. These problems tend to be more apparent at advanced stages of learning because of significant differences in the structure of complex and compound sentences and in the stylistics of the Polish and English languages.

Finally, there is a difference between Polish and English in that the subject is obligatory in English, while in Polish it can be indicated only by the form of the verb and is not indicated at all when non-finite verbs are used. The difference is most apparent when the subject is the first or second person singular and plural of personal pronouns, which are obligatory in the English language but are frequently omitted in Polish.

Conclusion

The differences in Polish and English languages outlined in this chapter are only a few of the significant ones. There are many other areas in which the two languages differ, but these are not within the scope of this book. The ones mentioned here, however, should be of assistance to Poles learning English as a second language and to anyone dealing with Polish people, either in the classroom or elsewhere.

Things to Think About

1. To what extent do you think a person's mother tongue interferes with their ability to learn another language?
2. Can the mother tongue be used constructively in the language learning process? If so, how?

CHAPTER FOUR

DEFINING SELF IN SOCIETY

There are significant similarities as well as differences in the way individuals are defined in Polish and in English speaking societies. This chapter will first look at aspects of official identity (that is, the way in which a person is officially defined in a society); second, the chapter will examine the individual's position in the general structure of a society; third, family structure and the role of its individual members will be looked at; and fourth, the chapter will look at the ways in which individuals relate to their friends. This chapter will also look at how all of these factors influence the way Poles communicate.

Official Identity

The information that a person is expected to supply to those in authority is different in Poland to that in all English speaking countries. One of the most apparent differences is that all Poles over the age of 18 must have an identity card, which is the most important document they possess. It is used extensively in all dealings individuals have with institutions to confirm their identity. Without the card, it is virtually impossible to conduct everyday activities.

The ID card was a sensitive issue when it was raised by the opposition groups during the Communist rule. At that time everybody had to carry their ID card with them at all times and they had to produce it on demand. If anyone failed to produce their ID card, the authorities had the right to arrest them and hold them without charge for up to 24 hours. Despite the opposition to the ID card, when the new government came to power in 1989, it was found to be an extremely useful document from the administrative point of view. Consequently, the card remained and is still used today as the main form of personal identification.

The ID card includes a person's name, current address, date of birth, occupation and ethnic origin. Most of this information is presented in a similar way to that used in English speaking countries. For example, first, family and sometimes middle names are used, the same components make up the address, the date of birth and age, and occupations and ethnicity are defined in the same fashion as in English. But, there are also several minor differences. Some family names reflect a person's sex, and in the address numbers appear in slightly different order to that used in English.

Names

In Poland, when people are asked to give their full name, they are expected to provide the first and family names and, in official documents, the initial or full middle name. As in English, Polish family names were coined from words denoting professions, status or physical features of ancestors. Unlike English names, however, Polish female family names derived from adjectives have a feminine ending, while the names of male members of the same family have a masculine ending. For example:

female: *Maria Kazimiera Kowalska*
male: *Jan Andrzej Kowalski*

Residential Addresses

Addresses in Polish and in English include the same information, but the positions of the word 'street', street number and post code are different. In Polish, the abbreviated form of 'street' (*ul.*) precedes the name of the street, and the number of the building appears after the name of the street. Where appropriate, this is followed by the letter 'm' and the number of the apartment. The post code is written before the place name. Thus, a typical Polish address would be written as follows:

W.P. Zofia Dudek   (title, first name, family name)
ul. Marsa 8 m. 91   (street name, street number, flat number)
03–903 Warszawa   (post code, place name)

Both private and official letters are organised similarly in Polish and in English, except that in Polish private letters an exclamation mark is used instead of a comma after the salutation (for example, 'Dear Janusz!').

---

1. What proof of identity is used in your country?
2. Is the information contained on this document different from that contained on a Polish identity card?
3. If there are any differences, what do you think might be the reason for these differences?

Individual's Position in Society

Despite the ideology of communism, a classless society did not eventuate during the five decades of the Communist rule in Poland. The old social hierarchy of lower, middle and upper classes was replaced by a social structure in which the ruling elite—members of the Communist Party and middle and upper management—enjoyed a superior social position. At the same time, the position of former aristocrats continued to be respected despite the fact that they had officially lost their status.

Among the communists and the aristocrats alike status assumed great importance. Because material wealth was generally unattainable, the importance of people's status and position was inflated. As a result, professional titles such as 'doctor' and 'professor', and titles which refer to positions in the workforce were and still are frequently used to address people. For example, a manager would be referred to as *panie kierowniku* (Mr Manager) and an accountant would be addressed as *pani księgowa* (Mrs Accountant). People from aristocratic background are often addressed in a more respectful manner than other people.

The scarcity of quality goods and services during the Communist era gave the distributors a high status in the society. However, the distributors lost their position of importance soon after the change of government in 1989 and the subsequent change to market economy. Goods and services became more readily available to those who had the funds to purchase them rather than influence with the distributors.

The elitist view of society according to which a person's ancestry and material, educational or professional status determine that person's social position and behavioural patterns is, however, as strong as ever in Poland. While in most developed democratic countries these attitudes have been slowly changing during the second half of the 20th century, the totalitarian system in Poland has actually strengthened elitist tendencies. It will be many years before they change.

Consequently, most Polish immigrants in countries where such attitudes are not prevalent continue to behave according to elitist way of thinking. Many of those who occupy a similar social position abroad to that which they occupied in Poland tend to be subservient in the presence of their superiors—employers, prominent figures, richer or better educated people—and rather authoritarian towards those in subordinate positions. Most Poles tend not to venture beyond what they perceive as their own social stratum. If they ever do—for example, if they are invited out by their employer—they tend to be shy and uneasy. Others, who enjoyed less material wealth but a definitely higher social status in Poland than in the country to which they have immigrated—for example, professionals and white collar workers who through circumstances have to work on the factory floor—find it hard to mix successfully with their workmates. Sometimes they harbour feelings of resentment towards people such as their employers who have status the immigrants themselves used to have in Poland. Thus, Polish immigrants who have the same social status as well as those who have a lower status than they used to have in Poland find it hard to adjust to life in a society which is, or is at least meant to be, an egalitarian rather than an elitist one.

The Family

Unlike the Western nuclear family, which usually consists of a husband, wife and children, the Polish family is an extended unit encompassing several generations. Not all of the extended family necessarily lives under the same roof. The people in this extended group are related both by blood—grandparents, brothers and sisters—and by marriage. We will first examine the relationships between different age groups within a Polish family and then briefly look at the Polish terms used for family relationships, which are much more numerous and diverse than those used in English.

Family Relationships

Family Structure and Responsibilities

Until they are ready to go to school at the age of six or seven, nothing except respect for their elders is expected from the children in a typical Polish family. During their school and university years, children are expected to put as much effort into learning as they can. They are therefore relieved of the need to work to earn money as long as they are studying, even if they are in their twenties. However, children are expected to help with household chores as they grow older, so that they are better prepared for independent life later. In practical terms this means that parents will, as a rule, fully support all their children until they finish their education.

As soon as children complete their education, they are expected to go to work and start contributing financially to the family. In this way they repay part of the debt they owe the family by supporting the next generation of youngsters. When they marry, however, the bulk of their income is used for themselves and their own children. At the same time, they can still rely on significant support from those older members of the family who are either still in the work force and can assist financially or, if retired, are physically fit enough to help by looking after the children and running the household. In fact, in most Polish households it is not the parents but the grandparents who spend most time with the children, irrespective of whether they actually live under the same roof or not.

The family members who contribute most to the family but receive the least are usually those who are over 40 years old but have not yet retired. They are usually financially independent and well established in their work. They are expected to continue supporting their children until they, the parents, retire and to use their influence outside the family to assist other members to get, for example, better jobs, better pay and better access to sought-after goods and services. Having almost finished preparing their own children for independent life, they take on the added responsibility of caring for the elderly, sick, lonely and physically handicapped family members.

In most cases all adults in the family help, and those who are most successful assist financially if necessary. Unless there is a need to put someone in specialist care, such as in the case of mental illness, it is very rare for Polish families to send their members to institutions, even if the families are living in countries where institutions such as retirement villages are an accepted way of life. Those who do so are considered by others to be cruel, especially if they are seen to be sufficiently well off to take care of the family member at home.

Most elderly family members who are able to, take care of the children and run the households of younger members of the family who work. In contemporary Poland this is not a matter of choice but of necessity, since salaries are low and few households can afford to live on one income. Moreover, the shortage and prohibitive cost of housing means that most young couples spend at least the first 10 years of their married life living with their parents or their in-laws. It will be interesting to see if this changes over the next two or three decades as the standard of living improves and people begin to have more choices in the way they organise their lives.

Family Ties

A family structure such as the one described above, in which most members are dependent on one another, could not survive the trials of time without strong ties that exist between the members. Indeed, emotional ties and solidarity between family members are dearly cherished in Polish society.

Like most Slavs, Poles are emotional people who are not afraid to show their feelings, especially those of love and friendship. This is particularly so within Polish families, where emotions are freely displayed through a lot of physical contact. Men and women alike are greeted with hugs and kisses, as are the children, who are also picked up and turned around. Everyone present usually comments on how much the children have grown since the last time. After the greetings are over there is constant physical contact between the family members. The children sit on their favourite uncle's or aunt's knees, whoever is toasted is also kissed, sympathetic or congratulatory embraces are shared if it is a sad occasion or if it is a celebration, and children are patted and kissed at every opportunity. The children in fact are constantly attended to and are frequently the centre of attention. Kisses and hugs are also exchanged on departure.

Family get togethers are a regular feature of Polish life, even if family members live far apart. This keeps emotional ties strong and provides regular opportunities for family matters to be discussed.

Most Polish families get together on Christmas Eve, when all members of the family living in the same vicinity gather, usually in the house of the most senior or most successful member of the family. They share a supper and wish each other well for the coming year. This occasion is important, so even family members from abroad try to attend it whenever they can. If they cannot, they are present symbolically. Poles customarily set one place at the table in case unexpected but welcome visitors come, be they family, close friends or lonely strangers.

Polish immigrants miss this contact with their families and many are therefore prepared to incur the cost of regularly travelling back to Poland. This may not be considered financially prudent by some other immigrants, who may not see even their closest family for over 10 years because they have other financial priorities. Polish immigrants, however, visit their relatives in Poland frequently and often bring out their families for prolonged visits.

Family Solidarity

Like family ties, solidarity is a very important binding force in Polish families. Family members from different households frequently help each other out, be it financially, emotionally or physically. They exchange information by letting each other know about opportunities in all walks of life, whether it is to do with availability of goods, job opportunities or ways of solving problems. Family solidarity is particularly apparent in difficult times, when family members rally behind those in need by offering financial assistance, supplying goods or helping out in the household. This was particularly apparent during and after World War II when the extremely difficult conditions strengthened rather than weakened family ties.

Family solidarity remains when Poles move to another country, not only among the immigrants themselves, but also with the families back in Poland. Immigrants usually continue to help their families in Poland in whatever way they can. In Sydney, for example, there were about 30 000 people of Polish extraction before the 1980s wave of immigration. At the same time, there were more than 10 firms whose main business was to organise the shipment of food parcels and transfer money to Poland. The amount of assistance sent to Poland became even greater after some 10 000 new immigrants arrived in the 1980s. Now, after the abolition of the Communist Government in 1989 and the introduction of a free market economy, these businesses are still booming. While the parcel traffic has decreased, difficult financial conditions prevailing in Poland have caused the mushrooming of businesses dealing in the transfer of money and making travel arrangements to and from Poland.

In Poland itself many Polish immigrants are now establishing businesses, often in cooperation with their families or close friends who had remained in Poland. Thus, while some foreign companies have invested in Poland, the economic reform and the growth that has followed has mainly been the result of the establishment by locals of small and medium-sized businesses which have strong connections with emigré Poles. The emigrés see this not only as a business investment, but also as a way of helping their families and assisting Poland as a whole.

Terms for Family Relationships

The large size of the extended Polish family and the strong emotional ties between its members are reflected in the large number and forms of terms used to denote family relationships. Polish has numerous terms for mother, father, grandparents, brothers and sisters, as well as terms to distinguish between various types of cousins.

The Polish word *kuzyn* does not refer to the children of one's aunts and uncles, as it does in English, but to the relationship between people whose grandparents are brothers and sisters. In other words, the Polish word refers to distant relatives, who are still considered to be close. As for the English word 'cousin', it has four different equivalents in Polish, which are used to refer to the children of one's uncles and aunts (as shown in Table 4.1 on the next page).

The qualifying adjectives (for example, *stryjecsny*) are often dropped, especially when the nature of the relationship is obvious. Thus, cousins are at times called *siostra* (sister) or *brat* (brother), emphasising the fact that cousins are close relatives. Many other forms are also used to denote other close relatives, reflecting the strong family ties.

Polish uses many more diminutives than English. Formal terms such as 'mother' (*matka*), 'father' (*ojciec*), 'grandfather' (*dziad*), 'grandmother' (*babka*), 'uncle' (*wuj*)

Table 4.1 Polish terms for cousins.

Polish term	Translation
stryjeczny brat	uncle's son (literally: brother on uncle's side)
stryjeczna siostra	uncle's daughter (literally: sister on uncle's side)
cioteczny brat	aunt's son (literally: brother on aunt's side)
cioteczna siostra	aunt's daughter (literally: sister on aunt's side)

and 'aunt' (*ciotka*) are rarely used in Polish, especially in informal situations. When addressing their parents, Polish children and adults alike use the words *mama* (Mum), *mamusia* (Mummy), *tata* (Dad), and *tatuś*. (Daddy). Grandparents likewise are not usually addressed by formal terms. They are the ones who usually spend most time with the children, give them the most love and attention and are almost invariably associated with the children's fondest memories. As a result, the formal word for grandmother does not exist in Polish, and equivalents for grandfather (*dziad*) and grandma (*babka*) are used only when referring to the ancestors. The words used to refer to grandparents are the diminutives *dziadek* (grandpa) and *babcia* (grandma). Likewise, uncles and aunts are usually referred to by diminutives such as *wujek* (uncle), *ciotka* (auntie) and *ciocia* (another diminutive of auntie).

1. How does the typical family in your country differ from the Polish family?
2. What impression do you think most Poles have of families in English speaking countries?
3. How would you explain family life in an English speaking country to your Polish friends or students?

Friendship

Terms for Friends

Any discussion of Polish customs concerned with friendship must begin with a comparison of words used in Polish and in English to describe these types of relationships. Their meanings and uses differ significantly in the two languages.

If we look up the words 'friend' and *przyjaciel* in an English–Polish dictionary, we will notice immediately the difference in the length and content of the two entries. The English word 'friend' is defined as 'close/best friend', 'mate', 'acquaintance', 'colleague' and 'comrade', while the Polish word *przyjaciel* is given only a single definition, 'close friend'. Polish, however, uses three other words which refer to friends, namely *kolega* (colleague or workmate), *znajomy* (acquaintance) and *towarzysz* (comrade). The three Polish words denote specific positions in the hierarchy of relationships. Close friends (*przyjaciele*) are at the top together with the most favoured family members, while colleagues and acquaintances are respectively on the two lower levels.

Kolega are a group of people who, at one time or another, shared some part of the day on a regular basis—people who were at the same school, studied at the same university, were in the same army unit or on the same sports team, and people who either have worked or are still working in the same place. The *kolega* type of friendships tend to be what is described in English as 'mateship'. It is within this group of people that close friendships develop most often. *Znajomy*, on the other hand, are people who meet only occasionally.

The third word, *towarzysz*, in pre-Communist times meant the same as 'mate'. Since the Communist takeover however, it has acquired the more sinister connotations of the word 'comrade', which developed as a result of the Russian Revolution and later the Cold War. Consequently, most Polish people consider *towarzysz* to be a negative term.

The different Polish words for friendship do not have precise equivalents in English and are used differently to their English translations. First, the English words 'acquaintance' and 'colleague' are not used frequently, and if they are used at all, it is to describe a relationship rather than to introduce someone. In other words, when a close friend, an acquaintance or a colleague is introduced in English, they are usually referred to as 'my friend [Mary]' or simply 'Mary'. In Polish, however, a close friend would be introduced as 'my close friend [Mary]' and an acquaintance as 'my acquaintance [Mary]'. Second, the word *kolega* has a wider use than the English word 'colleague'. It refers not only to another member of a profession, an associate or a coworker, but it also includes the meaning of 'mate'. Third, the word *przyjaciel* (close friend) is used reservedly to refer only to a few very special friends. Last, the word *towarzysz* is used now only among members of some leftist political groups and by ordinary Poles to speak negatively about former members of the Communist Party.

Close Friendship

Many English speakers tend to distinguish friendships according to sex, with 'mate' or 'buddy' typically referring to the masculine relationship and close friendships being more typical of women. The Polish concept of close friendship combines these two concepts. In Polish, it is completely irrelevant whether close friends are of the same or opposite sex.

Close friends enjoy a status similar to that of family members. They visit each other regularly, whether they are invited or not, they participate in discussions of matters which are usually kept private within the family and, like members of the family, they are expected to offer assistance if they can. There is a saying both in Polish and in English which reflects this relationship: *Prawdziwych przyjaciół poznajemy w biedzie*. (A friend in need is a friend indeed).

In Polish culture, close friendship is usually a very special and enthusiastically cultivated relationship. It is something to be proud of. Consequently, special friends behave towards each other differently in that they show affection for each other more readily, and they treat each other more favourably than they treat colleagues and acquaintances. At functions, special friends will often show preference for each other's company and even neglect others.

Forms of Address

Whenever communication occurs between people, be it in speech or in writing, a choice needs to be made as to the form of address to be used. The choice that is made depends on the kind of relationship the people involved have and on the situation they are in.

The repertoire of Polish terms of address is very similar to that in English. It includes the use of first names, the words that refer to family relationships—such as mum, dad, grandpa and auntie—the words *pan* (Mr or sir), *pani* (Mrs, Ms or Madam), *państwo* (Mr and Mrs) and a range of titles. Also, both English and Polish use such terms as *doktor* for medical practitioners and people with PhDs, and *profesor* for academics holding this position—although in Polish this term is also used for high school teachers.

Polish uses many more titles than English to denote people's position or profession, especially in the workplace and between providers of professional services and clients. Thus words such as *majster* (foreman), *kierownik* (manager), *dyrektor* (director) *sędzia* (judge) and *radca* (councillor) are used frequently. There is also a significant grammatical difference, that is, the second person of the verb is used only after first names or where use of the first name is implied. In all other situations the third person singular or plural of the verb must be used.

The main differences between English and Polish forms of address do not lie in the forms themselves however, rather in the way they are used. In English, when first names are used to address others, it is not possible to determine what the relationship of the participants is on the basis of the forms of address used. The same terms could be used at a family gathering, a work party, a party for the supporters of a local football team or even at a gathering of complete strangers linked only by the fact that they are attending the same function. Often name tags are given to people attending functions and conferences to help them participate more comfortably by using first names. Titles and family names are used only in formal or official situations.

In Polish, on the other hand, first names and second person singular or plural of the verb are used only among family members and very close friends. In other words, first names are used only to address people with whom the speaker is on intimate terms. The use of such titles as *pan, pani* and *państwo*, followed by the third person of the verb, is the most usual way of addressing other people, both strangers and those who are known to the speaker.

In Polish, age also determines the forms of address used. Children and teenagers use the familiar forms, the first name and the second person of the verb when they communicate with their peers, but it is not acceptable for them to use these forms when they address adults. Consequently, inside the family children use kinship terms such as *mama* (mum), *tata* (dad) and *ciocia* (aunt) to address their elders, and outside the family they use the words *pan* (Mr or Sir), *pani* (Mrs, Ms or Madam) and *państwo* (Mr and Mrs), followed by a verb in the third person. All adults, irrespective of whether they are relatives or not, address children and teenagers by their first name and the second person of the verb.

Virtually all adults use the words *pan, pani, państwo* and the third person of the verb to address people outside their circle of close friends and family. The only exceptions to this rule are groups such as conscript soldiers, sports teams and university students, who tend to become cohesive very quickly. Such groups use first names and the second person of the verb.

In private contacts and when talking to people on the same level at work, the words *pan, pani* and *państwo* are normally followed by the family name of the person when they are addressed for the first time. The third person of the verb is used throughout the conversation where speakers of English would use the personal pronoun 'you'. When addressing superiors at work, Poles will often use the title of the person being addressed rather than the family name—for example, *Panie kierowniku* (Mr Manager).

If a worker wishes to ask if Janek Kowalski has a pen, for example, the question would be asked as follows:

Czy ma pan pióro?

which literally translates to:

Has Mr got a pen?

This can be said less formally by using the first name instead of the family name, but the word *pan* still has to be used, as follows:

Panie Janku, czy ma pan pióro?
(Mr Janek, has Mr got a pen?)

If *Jan Kowalski* was addressed by a subordinate, the first name would never be used. Only the title would be used, as follows:

Czy ma pan pióro, panie kierowniku?
(Has Mr got a pen, Mr Manager?)

Thus, both Polish and English languages use titles and family names at formal occasions. Poles, however, use titles more often, especially when addressing their superiors. In informal situations, the forms of address used by the two languages differ significantly. Whereas native speakers of English tend to address everyone in the same way, Poles reserve the use of the first name and second person of the verb for their families and intimate friends.

Because in English first names and second person of the verb are used in most situations, it is more difficult to express respect for age and status, or to indicate the exact degree of familiarity. Consequently, English tends to vary the message in order to convey social differences. For example, a close friend who is talking too much could be told without offence:

'Oh, shut up, Jake!'

The same could be said by a parent to a child. However, this would not be an appropriate way for a school teacher to talk to a school pupil. Rather, what would be more appropriate in that situation would be:

'Stop talking Jacob!'.

Even this would be an unacceptable way of addressing a university student, who should be spoken to as follows:

'Could you please stop talking, John?'

If a lecturer wishes to interrupt the head of department, it would be more appropriate to say something like:

'Excuse me Keith, but may I say something?'

Note that in all cases the first name is used and that it is not the form of address that makes the message culturally acceptable.

In Polish, on the other hand, forms of address denote the level of respect and indicate the relative distance between speakers. The messages themselves do not need to be drastically modified to suit different situations. When peers are addressed either in formal or informal situations, frequent use of terms such as *pan*, *pani* and *państwo*, followed by the third person of the verb, emphasise respect and the polite character of the message. At work, superiors and professional people are addressed by their appropriate titles, thus acknowledging their status. For example, immediate superiors would be addressed as *panie majstrze* (Mr Foreman) or *pani kierowniczko* (Mrs Manageress), a judge would be addressed as *panie sędzio* (Mr Judge) and an accountant as *pani księgowa* (Mrs Accountant).

The use of first names and second persons of the verb when addressing adults is considered extremely impolite. However, people who have known each other since childhood continue to address each other by the familiar forms. When two adults become friends they can change from formal to informal ways of addressing each other, but this is of great significance and does not occur as a matter of course. It requires a declaration of intention and the consent of the other person. Usually, the initiative should be taken by the person who holds a higher social status. Thus, an older person should make the suggestion to a younger one, a woman to a man and a boss to the employee.

Finally, Polish unlike English has a great variety of diminutive forms which are used frequently within families and with friends. Since the second person of the verb is usually used to address family members and friends, imperative forms can be used in this context and, indeed, they are frequently employed when making requests or when advice is being given to a family member or a friend. Thus, it would be appropriate for a host to say to a friend during a party:

> *Przestań już opowiadać i siadaj do stołu Jasiu, trzeba coś zjeść.*
> (Stop telling stories Jan and sit at the table. It's time to eat.)

The English translation may sound somewhat abrupt, but in Polish it is perfectly friendly. Many Poles learning English tend to transfer into English the use of the imperative when they use first names, particularly if they are especially friendly with the person to whom they are speaking. Unfortunately, English speakers are likely to perceive this as being abrupt and perhaps even begin to think that Poles are usually very rude, not realising that it is simply a linguistic error.

---

1. How do you wish to be addressed by your Polish students and friends? Do you think this may pose problems for them?
2. How do you feel when people address you in ways you are not accustomed to?
3. How would you explain the use of the first name in English forms of address to your Polish friends or students?
4. Define the word 'friend'.
5. Do you think friendship is defined in Polish culture in the same way as it is in English speaking cultures? What similarities and what differences can you identify?

Things to Think About

1. In English, first names of friends tend to be shortened so that, for example, Joseph becomes Joe, Jacqueline becomes Jacky and Elizabeth becomes Liz. With the help of your English speaking friends, compile a list of 10 male and 10 female names which can be shortened.
   (a) When and by whom is it appropriate to use these shortened names?
   (b) Are these shortened names used as diminutives are used in Polish? How do they differ?
2. Do you feel more comfortable if the teacher uses your Polish name or if the English version is used? Discuss this matter in class with your teacher and other students.
3. Listen to people speaking English, to films and television to find out how people are addressed. The chart below lists names of people and their

relationship to you. In the third column of the chart write how these people should be addressed. The first has been completed for you. Check the answers with your teacher.

Name	Relationship	Form of address
Edward James Smith	friend	Ed
Jane Carol Perkins	doctor	
Thomas Lawson	your superior at work	
Mary Anne McPherson	woman colleague 20 years older than you	
Geoffrey Anderson	your teacher, a university professor	
Louise Anne Taylor	university professor you do not know personally	
Valerie Curtis	15 year old girl	
John David Couts	80 year old friend	
Douglas Paul Johnson	your accountant	

4. Draw up your family tree and write, in Polish, against each relative's name their relationship to you. Underneath, write the English equivalent.
   (a) Are there any Polish words for family relationships that are difficult to translate into English?
   (b) Ask an English speaking friend to draw up their family tree. Who do they consider to be members of their own family?
   (c) Are there any differences between what constitutes a family in Poland and what constitutes one in English speaking countries?
5. (a) What role do your grandparents play in your family? Do you think this is similar to other Polish families?
   (b) Ask an English speaking friend about their relation with their grandparents. What similarities and what differences are there between your relationship with your grandparents and your friend's relationship with theirs?
6. List five professions that are prestigious in Poland and five that are not. Ask two or three of your English speaking friends to make up similar lists for their countries.
   (a) Compare the lists. What are the most striking similarities and what are the differences?
   (b) Compare your results with those of others in your class. What are some of the reasons for the differences?
7. Below is a questionnaire on attitudes about families. Indicate in the boxes in the first column if you agree (A) or disagree (D) with each statement. Ask two other Polish people and three people from English speaking countries to likewise answer the questions.

Question	Poles			People from English speaking countries		
1. Parents should support their children until they complete their tertiary education.						
2. If a young couple are not able to buy their own home, their parents should invite them to live with them.						
3. If parents are better off than their children, they should help them financially.						
4. If the children are working, they should contribute financially to the household.						
5. Brothers and sisters should help financially family members who are less well off.						
6. Grandparents should help with caring of their grandchildren.						
7. When parents grow old and can no longer look after themselves, they should live in a retirement village.						
8. All important decisions should be discussed first with one's parents.						
9. All important decisions should be discussed first with one's brothers and sisters.						
10. Parents and children should maintain close contact and help each other.						

   (a) Are there any significant differences between the answers given by you and Poles and those given by people from English speaking countries?

   (b) What conclusions can you draw from these answers?

8. Below is a questionnaire on family relationships. Complete the questionnaire for yourself and then ask an English speaking friend to complete it also.

Question	You	Your friend
1. If you are no longer living with your parents (or with you children), how often do you see them?		
2. How many of your relatives, apart from your parents, grandparents brothers and sisters, do you see regularly?		

Question	You	Your friend
3. How often does your family have a family reunion?		
4. Would you expect family members to help you financially if you were in trouble?		
5. If they did help you, would you be expected to pay back the money?		
6. If you had a problem that could be solved by a relative who you do not know well, would you ask them for help?		
7. Do you think they would go out of their way to help you?		
8. If that same relative was a company director, would you expect your application for a job to be treated more favourably than those of other applicants?		
9. If you won a large sum of money, would you share it with members of your family?		
10. If you had a major problem, with whom would you most likely discuss it?		

    (a) What similarities and what differences are there in the answers?

    (b) Which answers do you find most interesting and why?

9. English speaking visitors to Poland often comment that in Poland people welcome others with open arms and friendships are very easily made. Poles living in English speaking countries, however, often claim that English speaking people do not have really close friends because they are too afraid to show their feelings. What do you think is the explanation for these two attitudes?

10. What does friendship mean to you?

    (a) Make a list of 10 qualities of what you consider to be a good friend, and ask an English speaker to do the same.

    (b) What differences and what similarities are apparent in the two lists?

CHAPTER ■ FIVE

LIVING IN SOCIETY

While the values, beliefs and patterns of behaviour of a given culture tend to change slowly, certain aspects of social life change much more quickly. This is especially true of the way people earn a living, housing, how goods and services are acquired, transportation and leisure. In Poland it is likely that some of these specific aspects will change drastically because of the changes the country is currently experiencing. However, these changes remain part of Poland's established culture, the influence of which is likely to be felt for some time to come.

Earning a Living

Until 1989 the labour market in Poland was similar to that of other communist countries in that there was virtually full employment and jobs were relatively permanent even though wages were low. Most school leavers and university graduates were guaranteed jobs, and in some cases were required to work for up to three years with specific enterprises. Various government enterprises offered scholarships or they offered employment to senior secondary school students and those completing university studies. Some students remained in the enterprises that employed them in the first place, while others later looked for different jobs with help from friends or other personal contacts. Only sometimes would they acquire a new job by responding to advertisements.

Prior to 1989, if an enterprise reduced its employee numbers or even closed, the layed-off staff did not usually become unemployed. Either the employer or government agencies made sure that all those who had lost their jobs were offered new positions elsewhere or were retrained for new jobs. In practical terms this meant that in the majority of cases job applications were a formality and very few jobs were filled on competitive basis. The positions that were filled on competitive basis were mainly jobs in higher education and in research institutes.

Since the change of government and introduction of a market economy the labour market has been changing rapidly. Many Poles are still adjusting to this new situation in which a growing number of employers are private. Today, getting a job depends much more on qualifications, and keeping that job depends on performance and the financial viability of the enterprise.

Young school and university leavers have adjusted remarkably well to the new situation. However, people in their forties and fifties, particularly those living in smaller towns where the changes are slower, find it very hard to adjust. They have spent all their professional lives in state-owned enterprises and now find it difficult to find or create jobs in the Western way. These people make up the bulk of the long-term unemployed and have little hope of acquiring a well paid job in the near future. Many cherish the old fallacies about life in the Western countries and many of them join queues of applicants for immigration.

Most of these people are well qualified. Often the reason they have lost their job is because their place of work had closed, not because they were dismissed for poor performance. As a result, they are attractive potential immigrants and a number of them succeed in obtaining entry into developed countries. However, job searches in those countries are the same as they are now in Poland, in that job seekers must have the ability to find right jobs and apply for them in a competitive manner. Unfortunately, many of these immigrants do not have the skills to do this. Consequently, they not only need to learn English—although many already have knowledge of the language—but they also need to be trained in how to look for jobs, write application letters, compile resumés and handle interviews.

Looking for a Job

Many new arrivals from Poland are people who have already failed to secure a well paid job in Poland because of the newly introduced competition for jobs. It is highly likely then that without assistance these people will remain unemployed for a considerable length of time. The problems faced by blue collar workers are different from those encountered by white collar workers and professionals, and therefore will be discussed separately.

Acquiring unskilled blue collar jobs in Poland is relatively simple. People seeking work either use the services of a government employment agency or inquire directly. They can also answer advertisements placed in newspapers by small businesses and private individuals. There is, in fact, very little difference in the way people look for unskilled jobs in Poland and in any of the English speaking countries, except that in most English speaking countries there are private employment agencies as well as the government ones. Unskilled immigrants from Poland are therefore likely to face fewer problems in finding a job than their skilled and professional colleagues. They may only need information about the employment agencies and how to use them, and they may need to acquire a basic level of occupational English.

The situation for skilled blue collar workers is, however, more complicated. In Poland until recently young people who completed appropriate courses were virtually guaranteed a job and their career was secured for life. The move to a market economy, however, has changed this. Young job seekers now find themselves competing with experienced workers, who, like the young job seekers, lack many of the skills necessary to compete. Moreover, skilled workers who emigrate may have difficulties with their qualifications not being recognised, lack of familiarity with work practices in the new country and with the demands of job application process.

The professionals find it most difficult to secure a job in a new country. Their usual language problems are often compounded by the fact that many countries do not recognise foreign qualifications. Thus, a Polish physician, lawyer, accountant or computer specialist may be required to repeat at least a part if not the whole course of studies to be recognised in the host country. Such studies require time, money and a considerable knowledge of English, and may force the skilled professionals to work on assembly lines, drive taxis or do other unskilled labour for the first few years after their arrival.

This change from the top of the social ladder in Poland to the very bottom in the host country is traumatic for many and one that compounds the experience of cultural shock. Furthermore, having to adjust to the new country, work at menial labour and study at the same time makes effective study difficult. Even when the qualifications are obtained, these immigrants face yet another problem: unfamiliarity with the process of applying for a job.

Applying for a Job

In pre-1989 Poland job advertisements were generally short, with few specifications. This was because most appointments requiring selection committees were made by a panel which included the manager, the personnel officer and the leader of the Communist Party organisation in the enterprise. All three were party members and, in fact, political views and membership of Communist Party were considered as important as skills when making a selection. Selection was also based on the contacts the applicant had with the members of the appointing committee. In other words, personal contacts were of great importance in obtaining jobs. In fact, appointments were often decided even before advertisements were placed in newspapers.

When reading newspaper advertisements for jobs, Polish immigrants are likely to focus only on the formal qualifications required. They often ignore other specified requirements, such as 'team player', 'self-starter' and 'ability to work independently'.

Resumés

Polish immigrants also often have difficulty in compiling their resumés. They tend to write resumés that focus on educational qualifications and do not include details of specific positions previously held and responsibilities carried out. They may also be unaware of the importance of a well presented resumé in securing an interview.

The Job Interviews

The job interview itself is the final and most difficult hurdle for Polish immigrants. This is well illustrated by O'Grady and Moore (1994) who describe the experience of Anna, a recently arrived immigrant to Australia. During an interview for a position as a chemical engineer, Anna was asked why she had applied for the job. She replied that she wanted to work in her chosen profession. She had looked and found a job in which she could use the qualifications she had from Poland, and that is why she was there. Being unaware of the purpose of interviews in English speaking countries, Anna did not understand the question as an invitation to show how her qualifications and, even more importantly, her experience related to the needs of the company. She consequently missed the opportunity to highlight her abilities.

Interviewers are likely to consider such a response to be an indication of a lack of interest and long-term commitment to the company. Applicants such as Anna are likely to be judged as unreliable from the companies point of view because the applicants seem concerned only with themselves and not with the needs and interests of their potential employers. In Anna's case, this impression was probably reinforced when she went on to say, regarding the specific position, that she had done this work before and that she did not think she would need to know more about it. She said that they needed a chemical engineer and she was a chemical engineer.

Anna saw the interview solely as an opportunity to verify her qualifications and did not realise that the interviewing panel was also looking for someone who was interested in the company itself and had desirable qualities such as initiative and ability to work in a team. Responses such as these are likely to be seen as arrogant and a sign of inflexibility.

Many Poles may also find it difficult to highlight their own abilities. Klos Sokol (1994) describes one such example:

> I had heard a friend was very successful at her new job with a pharmaceutical company so I congratulated her. Horrified, she responded, 'Oh no, please don't say that. Anyone could do this job—and besides, I really don't know what I'm doing.' Talking about her achievements seemed so painful for her, I was almost sorry that I mentioned it. (p. 22)

---

1. (a) What sort of qualities do companies in English speaking countries look for in their employees?
   (b) Which of these are likely to give your Polish students difficulty?
   (c) How would you prepare your students for an interview for a job in a company in an English speaking country?
2. If you were asked to prepare a lecture for immigrants on how to look for a job in Australia or any other English speaking country, what points would you cover?

Career Development

The policy of full employment of the Communist Government in Poland meant that once people were employed in an organisation, their career development proceeded within that same organisation. For most Poles this usually meant that they progressed up the salary and responsibility ladder until they reached the level normally reserved either for members of the Communist Party or for people trusted by it. In other words, non-party members could only reach a relatively low threshold of responsibility and salary, involving the supervision only of a small group of people.

Significant leaps up the ladder within the same organisation or attainment of higher positions by changing employers did not occur frequently for the majority of the workforce, and qualifications did not necessarily play an important part in the process. In fact, the only way to develop one's career was to join the Communist Party. The Communist Party had therefore some capable people in its ranks because once employees reached decision-making levels they could not progress further without joining the party. However, people with inferior qualifications who joined the party and became active members were also able to advance more quickly than others. It was mainly these people who filled the higher managerial positions in education, the public service and the manufacturing and service industries. They were the so-called *nomenklatura*—a group of trusted party members who were the powerful elite and who had the exclusive right to fill all available managerial positions. They were resented by those who, despite being better qualified, occupied lower positions. Consequently, the notion of a career gradually acquired a negative meaning, and words such as *karierowicz* (careerist) were used to describe people who had gained better positions and financial benefits as a result of lack of moral principles rather than genuine ability.

Many Poles have known only this negative aspect of career development and find it difficult to look at it in the positive light, whether they still live in Poland or abroad. Some well qualified and experienced people spend a long time working in one place on production lines or in submanagerial positions not only because they do not know how to apply for jobs properly, but also because they often fail to realise that their employers are quite prepared to consider requests for advancement. Thus, these immigrants fail to make the right move at the right time.

---

1. What do you understand by the term 'career'?
2. What advice would you give a highly qualified person from Poland to help them develop their career in Australia or any other English speaking country?

Establishing a Business

Unlike in most other Eastern Block countries, private businesses existed in Poland throughout the post-war period. However, this was only on a small scale as government policies severely limited the scope of private business activities and profits. The small number of people who owned their own businesses had to devote a lot of their effort to concealing their profits, because taxation policies discouraged large-scale private developments and enforced one-of taxes on successful business people whenever there were shortfalls in the state budget. As a result, many of the small businesses were almost permanently threatened with bankruptcy and only the smartest tax evaders survived in the long run. Many used the first available opportunity to defect to the West and establish businesses there, while others remained to survive somehow. Both groups are now contributing to the development of a free market economy in Poland. A number of business people who emigrated are returning to invest in businesses in Poland, and those who managed to survive under the Communist Government are now rapidly expanding their existing enterprises.

In communist Poland there were also many small, unofficial businesses which operated 'on the side'. Because these types of businesses were not registered, it is difficult to estimate the number of people involved. This was typical not only in Poland, but also in many other Eastern Block countries where goods and services were hard to get. There were not enough official private businesses to satisfy demand and state owned enterprises were unreliable, inefficient and unwilling to provide goods and services to individuals. Thus, everyone knew that the plumber who came to fix the dripping radiator in the evening was using materials stolen from the state-owned enterprise where he worked during the day, and that the electrician and the carpenter did likewise. The goods and services acquired in this way cost a little more but often this was the only way to get things done efficiently.

Now, even though there are numerous opportunities for businesses to be established legally, change is very slow. This is mainly due to the fact that until recently most small business enterprises were either based on partly dishonest practices—such as trading of stolen parts—or operated on the basis that the running of an unofficial small business involved few costs and little risk. In other words, most Poles have had very little real business experience and do not know how to go about establishing a successful business in a competitive environment. As a result, the majority of recent Polish immigrants tend to seek employment rather than start their own businesses. Very few of them develop successful businesses of their own.

Things to Think About

Read carefully the advertisements below and answer the questions that follow.

1. Read the advertisements on pp. 56–7.
   (a) Identify the key words in each advertisement and then list the characteristics which are mentioned most often.
   (b) How would you use:
      (i) your letter of application;
      (ii) your resumé; and
      (iii) the interview
   to convince prospective employers that you actually have the qualities and qualifications they are looking for?
2. Chose one of the advertisements on pp. 56–7.
   (a) Form half the class into teams of three to interview applicants for that job. The interviewing panel should decide on a series of questions each applicant is to be asked and the answers it expects from successful applicants.
   (b) Divide the remaining students into groups of three to prepare themselves for the interview. Each group should predict what questions are likely to be asked.
   (c) Each interviewing panel is then to interview three of the students individually and decide who will be offered the job and why.
   (d) Each panel is to present its decision to the class together with the reasons for its decision.
3. Choose one of the jobs advertised on pp. 56–7.
   Write a letter of application for the job and compile a resumé. Ask your teacher or an English speaking friend to check it for you.
4. The following questions are often asked at interviews in English speaking countries:
      (i)   Why do you want this job?
      (ii) What are your strong points in relation to this job?
      (iii) What are your weak points in relation to this job?
      (iv) This job involves a considerable amount of team work. Are you a team player?
      (v)   This job is stressful. Do you think you can handle it?
   (a) For each of the above questions, what answer do you think the prospective employer is looking for?
   (b) How would you answer each of these questions?
5. If a foreigner was looking for a job in Poland, what advice would you give them? Write a letter to a friend giving them advice on how to get a job in Poland.

Acquisition of Goods and Services

Housing

Most city dwellers in Poland live in drab multi-storey blocks, which are characteristic of all former communist countries in Eastern Europe. During World War II, before the Communists took over, most houses and apartment blocks were destroyed or damaged. In Warsaw, for example, 80 per cent of buildings were destroyed. A government housing policy was therefore necessary to provide accommodation for everyone. As a result, during the first 20 years of Communist rule all housing was controlled totally by the state housing authority. People were allocated flats, rooms in larger flats or very occasionally houses, depending on their position and the size of their family.

Despite this government policy, a lack of housing remained the big problem of the 1945-88 period. While most people were able to save enough money for a deposit, the government was unable to erect enough new homes to meet the demand. As a result, many young people had to wait for up to 20 years after they paid the deposit to actually move into their new flat. It was always an important reason for saving and a prominent issue that was constantly addressed by party leaders and discussed in the media and in private conversations. Lack of housing even inspired art, songs about the 'little dream flat' and plays about the cramped living conditions in flats accommodating two or three generations which created conflicts. Since early payment of the deposit meant that people would join the queue sooner, many parents began saving for their children's flats even before they started school. In short, the housing problem was constantly on people's minds.

Tenants Cooperatives and Other Forms of Housing in Poland

In the late 1950s, new forms of housing were introduced, one of which was tenants cooperatives which were owned and controlled by the state. People wishing to obtain a flat in such a cooperative had to pay a substantial deposit and a monthly rent which covered maintenance and heating costs. The advantage of this over-subsidised government housing was that families renting the flats could not be moved to other accommodation unless they themselves chose to do so. Also, if the main tenant of the flat died, remaining family members living in the flat had the right to stay there as long as they payed a new deposit.

There was at that time a growing number of people who wished to own the flats in which they lived so that they could sell them or pass them on to members of their immediate family in case of death. For them, the government began a scheme similar to strata title blocks in Australia, the only difference being that the government rather than private owners initially owned the buildings. Each apartment in a block had a specific price and people who wished to buy one paid a deposit and borrowed the rest of the money from the government. They then paid not only the rent, which covered maintenance and heating costs, but also instalments on the mortgage, which was usually given for a 20–25 year term. After the mortgage was paid off, the flat was fully owned and could be sold, rented out or inherited by relatives.

Since the collapse of the Communist Government, the status of the tenant's cooperatives has remained unresolved. However, existing owner cooperatives have become fully independent and many new ones are being established by private investors rather than by the government.

Buying Real Estate

For Poles, a free-standing house or a townhouse with a garden is the ultimate dream. Housing in Poland is now being taken over by the private sector, but even so it will be sometime before the housing situation is rectified. Consequently, owning a free-standing house is and will be for quite some time an unattainable goal for most people in Poland. The opportunity to own one's own home, therefore, remains one of the great attractions of Western countries. In fact, the desire to own a house rather than a flat is so strong that many Polish immigrants prefer to buy a house in an outer city suburb far from their place of work rather than purchase for the same price an apartment closer to work and the city centre.

Immigrants thinking of buying a house may not be aware of some of the pitfalls of investing in real estate. First, in Poland, location does not play as important a part as it does elsewhere, and a house is often more expensive than the land. Poles, therefore, tend to consider the value of the house itself the most important factor in determining the price and they tend to, as a result, invest in a large house in a poor location. Second, until now, banks in Poland did not lend money for buying real estate. Apartments were built by the state and repayments were made to the government. Free-standing houses and townhouses had to be purchased outright. As a result, many Polish immigrants wait until they have a sizeable deposit before they start looking for a house and approach banks for mortgages. Also, because until recently the value of Western currencies was very high in Poland, the idea of borrowing sums as large as $100 000 is frightening to Polish immigrants, even if their income can support the mortgage.

Renting

The scarcity and government control of housing in Poland meant that private renting was virtually non-existent in the big cities. Furthermore, residence in big cities such as Warsaw, Cracow and Gdańsk was controlled. All residents had to register and people from outside these city areas were prevented from moving into such cities unless an employer applied for a change of residence on their behalf. Most employers were reluctant to do this because if they did so, they were also responsible for providing housing for the new employees. The construction of a new factory in a large city was usually accompanied by building of company workers' accommodation close by. All this discouraged the development of a private rental market.

Most Poles have to wait a long time to obtain an apartment or house, whether

Things to Think About

1. The table below compares household expenses in Poland with similar expenses in an English speaking country. Complete the section relating to Poland and ask a person from an English speaking country to complete the second section. Write the name of that country at the top of column three.

Expense	Poland			
	Amount	% of monthly income	Amount	% of monthly income
Rent Electricity Gas/coal Food Transport				

Which of the items listed differ significantly between the two countries and which are roughly the same?

2. Read the comments below and then list some of the reasons why many people in English speaking countries prefer buying a house to renting one.

As soon as they complete their education and start working, most Westerners start thinking seriously about buying a flat or a house of their own. They know that living in rented accommodation means constantly rising costs and that they may be asked to leave at relatively short notice. What is more, all the money they spend disappears in someone else's pocket.

If home buyers borrow money from a bank and buy their own unit or house, they still have to pay quite a lot each month, maybe even more than if they were renting, but this payment goes to pay off the interest and loan they have taken from the bank to buy the property. In other words, the money they are paying no longer disappears, but rather it works for them and, eventually, after the loan is paid off, the flat or house they are living in will be theirs.

There are some big advantages in paying off a loan rather than renting. Because of inflation, rents rise every now and then—they never go down or stay the same for more than a year or two. In other words, after 10–15 years renting, the tenants may be paying up to twice as much as they were paying at the outset for the same accommodation. A mortgage is different. While initially monthly repayments may be quite a burden for the family, especially during the first few years, they do not rise significantly (unless interest rates rise), and so they become less and less of a burden. In fact, many people pay off their mortgage early.

3. Do you think it is better to buy or to rent? Could you buy a house in the near future? Do these exercises to find out if you could.

   (a) How much a month do you pay in rent?

   (b) Find out how much money you can borrow from a bank if you were to pay the same amount for mortgage as you are paying in rent. Add 5 per cent deposit to the sum you can borrow from a bank and you will have the price of the house you can afford.

   (c) Look up the real estate advertising section of a newspaper and find out what you can buy within that price range.

4. Having done the above exercise, do you think you are better off renting or buying a house? Explain why.

5. Three houses within your price range were advertised last week. Read carefully the descriptions of the houses, then answer the questions that follow.

   House No. 1

   An old three-bedroom fibro house on a block of land (1000 square metres). The house needs to be fixed inside, and the garden has not been maintained very well. The house is located only 5 minutes by car from your place of work. All other houses in the street are quite modern and made of brick, and some of them are large. In fact, the advertised house is in the worse condition than any other house in the street.

   House No. 2

   A new three-bedroom townhouse with a small yard. It is close to a major road and there is some noise, but it is within walking distance of your place of work.

   House No. 3

   A beautiful modern four-bedroom house with an in-ground pool in lovely bush setting, close to school and a railway station. It is located in an outer suburb, an hour's drive and 45 minutes train ride from your place of work.

   (a) Which of the three houses would be most suitable for you and your family? Give reasons for your choice.

   (b) Which of the three houses would be the best investment for the future? Why?

   (c) Which one would you choose and why? Give reasons for your choice.

owned or rented. They, therefore, tend to remain at the same address for most or all of their lives. Consequently, when they come to a country such as Australia, the most frequent misconception they have about rented accommodation is a false sense of security. Rapid changes in rental prices and requests from owners to vacate premises with only a few weeks notice may take them by surprise. Some may avoid buying in the belief that renting is equally secure.

Shopping

Until the introduction of a free market economy, shopping in Poland used to be a major challenge involving considerable time and skill to find where and when goods were going to be delivered and then to know which queues to line up in—especially to purchase more expensive items such as furniture and home appliances. Even buying everyday necessities such as food required lining up for hours.

All this has changed now and even though many things are still not produced locally, goods are imported to satisfy demand. The queues have disappeared and people no longer buy whatever is available but rather what they need. People also no longer hoard excessive quantities of goods—in case of shortages—as they used to do until recently.

The quality of service has also changed. Until recently, shop assistants in government department and specialty stores were the distributors of sought-after goods and often behaved in a patronising or authoritarian manner towards their customers. This was in marked contrast to owners of private shops where service was fast and polite. After the change of government in 1989, the retail industry was the first to be totally privatised. Today all shops in Poland are privately owned.

The main differences between shopping in Poland and in Western countries are the quality and type of services offered. In Poland, most food, for example, is still bought in small corner shops rather than in supermarkets. Credit facilities are not widely available.

New arrivals from Poland tend to find the limited opening hours of some shops an inconvenience, because in Poland all shops are open from 6 am to 7 pm. Also, the speed of service and the fact that shop assistants serve only one customer at a time can be irritating. In Poland, whenever there was a delivery of goods to the shops, sales staff had to deal with large number of impatient customers and they simply had to operate quickly and efficiently, sometimes serving up to three customers at a time. The queues have now disappeared but the speed of service has not changed. It is not surprising then that people arriving from Poland may get annoyed at seeing a shop assistant waiting while one customer is taking time to decide what to buy. Furthermore, shop assistants, especially in department stores, often seem to know very little about the products they are selling. Shop assistants in Poland, on the other hand, will often demonstrate considerable knowledge about a particular product and will often talk the client into buying it.

Things to Think About

The questionnaire below has been designed to compare shopping in Poland and in an English speaking country. First, answer the questions yourself by placing the answers in the 'Poland' column, then ask an English speaking friend to do likewise by putting the answers in the last column. Write the name of your friend's country at the top of that column.

Question	Poland	
1. How many days a week are shops open?.		
2. What time do most shops open?		
3. What time do most shops close?		
4. How many times a week do people go shopping?		
5. Do you do most of your shopping in small shops, supermarkets or in discount stores?		
6. Where you shop, do shop assistants serve one person at a time or more than one?		
7. Do shop assistants know a lot about the products they are selling?		
8. Would you describe those shop assistants as efficient?		

(a) Compare your results with those of other students. What are some of the similarities and what are the differences?

(b) Compared with the English speaking country you surveyed, what are the advantages and disadvantages of shopping in Poland?

Banks and Other Financial Institutions

Prior to 1989, the banking industry in Poland was fully owned by the state. It was possible to open a bank account in Poland—whether this was an ordinary savings, home savings or cheque account—and have one's salary paid into it. Banks could also arrange the automatic payment of regular monthly bills. However, bank loans were virtually non-existent and so people had to save or borrow from family or friends if they wanted to buy any of the more expensive items. Today, the policy of the government is to change the banking system slowly and not to allow credit industry to develop on large scale until the high inflation is brought under control.

Car and home insurance industry is well established and is now being privatised. However, the concept of superannuation as a source of additional income after retirement is completely unknown in Poland. The present government is continuing the traditional policy of fully funding pensions for women over 60 and men over 65. It has no policies on superannuation funds, nor has it restricted any arrangements private individuals may wish to make for additional income after they retire.

While most Poles are familiar with savings accounts and paying by cheque, they are not familiar with some of the more modern financial services and investment opportunities available in the West. As a result they may be either over-cautious or not careful enough when taking loans, using credit cards or investing their savings in shares or bonds. This situation is likely to change as financial services in Poland become more sophisticated.

Things to Think About

Imagine that you have $5000 to invest. Go to several financial institutions, such as banks, building societies, investment trusts and insurance companies, to inquire about the possibility of investing this sum for two years.

(a) Which institution offers the best rate of return for your investment?

(b) Compare your findings with those of other students.

Health

The National Health Service in Poland has been fully funded by the government for the last 50 years, with mixed results. While there are excellent teaching and clinical hospitals in large cities and very capable specialists who are part of international research programs, the system as a whole has never been very efficient.

The system provides basic health care for everyone, but the doctors, nurses and other support staff are overworked and underpaid, having to look after more patients than they should. To improve this situation, in the 1960s the government permitted the creation of medical cooperatives. The services provided by these cooperatives had to be paid for, but patients did not have to wait as long, doctors could spend more time with each patient and test results were returned more quickly. The new government has decided to continue funding the National Health Service in its entirety, but it has at the same time relaxed regulations relating to private practices and private hospitals.

Poles have an entirely different attitude towards health and sickness to people from most English speaking cultures. Most Poles consider health problems to be a private matter, and they do not discuss them with anyone except the closest family and friends. This attitude is particularly apparent in the doctor-patient relationship. Doctors in Poland do not usually discuss with the patients the details of their ailment before prescribing medicine as they often do in other countries. This is not because they do not have time or concern for their patients, but because most patients simply do not expect this. Doctors in Poland also do not tend to discuss with their patients alternative treatments. Patients there usually expect to be simply told what they are suffering from and then to be given the best possible treatment. They are not prepared to question the doctor's judgment, nor to have any input into medical decisions, other than when their consent for an operation is required.

Serious illnesses, especially of a life-threatening nature, are something Polish patients do not necessarily want to be fully aware of. This stems from the conviction that a positive attitude is as important in the healing process as medication, and that when the patient is told that their illness is incurable, they will suffer from depression which will only worsen their condition.

If a doctor in Poland discovers that a patient has developed a minor ailment, that ailment will be identified for the patient and appropriate medication will be prescribed. If, however, the problem is a serious one, a Polish doctor will usually tell the patient that it is difficult to say what the problem is and that some tests may be necessary. Later, the doctor will contact the patient's nearest relative and discuss the matter to determine what the patient should be told.

Because in English speaking cultures doctors are usually frank with their patients, Polish immigrants may be surprised when their doctor openly discusses with them the details of their health problem. Many would prefer to have a choice as to whether they hear the bad news or not.

Family and friends will usually refrain from discussing serious illness openly in the presence of the patient. The general attitude will be sympathetic and optimistic until the patient realises that their illness is incurable. Even then most Polish people will continue to pretend that something might be done, so that hope is not lost until the end. As a result, some patients even die without fully realising the seriousness of their condition. There are many cases of people having died without having settle their affairs.

Things to Think About

1. Find out about the health care system and health insurance in at least one English speaking country by asking a friend from such a country or writing to the appropriate embassy.
   (a) How does that system compare with the Polish system?
   (b) Discuss the strengths and weaknesses of each system with the rest of the class.
2. Doctors in English speaking countries feel it is their duty to discuss in detail their patient's illness and proposed treatment. Do you feel comfortable with this approach? Why/why not?
3. If you contracted a life-threatening illness, would you like your doctor to tell you about it? Discuss your views on the subject with the rest of the class.
4. What do you think people from English speaker countries feel about this issue?

Transport

The most common way of getting around in Polish cities is still by public transport, although an increasing number of people prefer to drive their own car or motorcycle. Travel between cities and villages is also done mostly by public transport, as well as in private cars and on motorcycles. The relatively short distances between cities (on average 200–300 kilometres) do not encourage air travel, especially because it is expensive.

By far the most common forms of public transport in the cities are buses and trams, which usually cover whole cities thoroughly. It is therefore possible to travel in a Polish city comfortably and quickly without a car or motorcycle. This is not so in the country, however, where public transport is less frequent.

Traffic in Poland moves on the right-hand side of the road. Traffic regulations have been standardised so that they are virtually the same as those in other European countries and in America. In Poland people do not tend to drive defensively, are less forgiving and can be aggressive when overtaking or telling slow drivers off.

There are good city maps and maps of country areas available in Polish book-shops. However, should anyone get lost, Poles are usually helpful to strangers and will assist travellers to find their way.

Leisure

Sports and Tourism

The difficult living conditions that prevailed in Poland over the last 50 years have not prevented people from enjoying their leisure time. Outdoor activities are very popular and tend to be similar to those enjoyed buy other Europeans. In summer, the beach is the most popular place for a day's outing, be it at the seaside or by rivers and lakes. The Baltic coast and the Lake District in the north are the most popular destinations for holiday makers with children. Sailing is also a very popular summer activity, as are camping, fishing, hiking and riding on pushbikes or motor-cycles in nature reserves and state forests.

Like most other Europeans, Poles ski and skate a lot. The temperatures drops below zero for long periods in winter, bringing with them plenty of snow and ice. As soon as the snow falls, open-air skating rinks are used in parks, on school sporting fields and on ponds. In the southern mountains there are hundreds of skiing resorts catering for everyone from the rich to the less wealthy.

1. What role does sport play in your country?
2. How does it compare to the role of sport in Poland?
3. How would you explain the role of sport in your country to a Polish friend?

Functions, Parties and Celebrations

Poles like to get together with friends and relations to celebrate weddings, anniversaries and when babies are baptised. They also celebrate birthdays, especially children's ones, but name days—the day dedicated to the saint after whom a person is named—are more important occasions for adults. Thus, while many of the occasions are similar to those celebrated in most English speaking countries, there are differences in the way these occasions are celebrated and in social interaction that take place at them.

For Poles, Christmas Eve is the most important family day of the year. On that evening the whole family gathers in the house of its leading or most senior member, a wafer blessed in church is shared by all and good wishes are exchanged. Christmas Eve supper consisting of 12 meatless dishes is eaten, but not before all members of the family who have quarrelled or held grudges against each other have reconciled. A set place is left for absent members of the family or for anyone who is alone and would like to share the supper with the family. That place is often filled. After the supper, Christmas presents are exchanged, unlike in some countries where gifts are given on Christmas Day.

On Christmas Eve many Polish immigrants inevitably feel homesick. In countries such as Australia, at Christmas time there is no snow, fragrant pine Christmas trees are not common and most of their families and close friends are far away. Telephone calls to Poland are difficult to make in the early hours of Christmas Day—Christmas morning in Australia is the evening of the previous day in Poland—as lines to Poland tend to be very busy with almost every Polish family in Australia trying to reach their relatives gathered for Christmas Eve supper. Since they cannot be with their families, most Poles want at least to make telephone contact. To Poles, Australians do not seem to make very much fuss of Christmas.

New Year's Eve is also celebrated differently in Poland. People in most English speaking countries tend to celebrate the arrival of the New Year on the evening of the 31 December and the celebrations usually end soon after midnight. In Poland, most adults either go out to New Year balls or organise private parties which include dancing. The celebrations usually begin about 10 pm and the first hour or so is devoted to eating, talking and getting acquainted with others at the party. This continues until midnight. At the stroke of 12, New Year toasts are drunk and then the parties and balls begin in real earnest. They continue until the morning of the New Year's Day.

Foreigners who happen to be in Poland on New Year's Day are often bewildered by the celebrations. The streets and country roads become crowded on New Year's morning with rowdy groups returning home. From 8 am onwards most adults sleep, children play with their grandparents and the country comes to a standstill.

Like most other people, Poles like to celebrate by eating with their families and friends. However, they tend to organise their parties differently and, due to climate, hold them mostly indoors. It is customary to be half an hour to an hour late for a party. Irrespective of whether it is a quick visit or a long evening party, it is never stated when the function will finish. People who are invited for a brief visit are usually asked to come in the evening on a week day or between 3 and 4 pm on weekends. At dinner and dancing parties, when cake and coffee are served it means that the party is almost over, but it is impolite to state the time the party is to finish or to tell guests that the party is over and they should leave. In Poland, therefore, it is not possible to have one set of people for a cocktail party in the early evening and then have a dinner party with a few select friends a little later, as the finishing times for functions are not specified.

Young people's parties usually include dancing and snacks set out on side tables. Parties for older people also include dancing, but everyone is seated at tables laden with food.

The custom of 'bringing a plate' is virtually unknown in Poland. The hosts are expected to provide everything: the venue, elaborate homemade food and drinks. The guests express their appreciation by bringing freshly cut flowers or a bottle of vodka, wine or champagne, and are expected to reciprocate with an invitation in the near future when they will likewise provide lavish food. This may be a problem for some non-Polish people, as one American reflected:

> I have only one problem with spending marvellous evenings at Polish friends' homes for parties, dinners, or drinks. I should reciprocate more often. Gulp. Confession: hosting Poles intimidates me. Can my hosting style ever match theirs? Poles will pile your plate over with pork chops ('We slaughtered our pet pig just for your visit!'), handmade pierogi ('Granny's arthritis doesn't stop her when it comes to guests!'), and homemade jams ('Threw my back out picking these strawberries!'). Even for a casual get-together, the right types of consumables appear. (Klos Sokol 1994, p. 71)

Very few big parties are organised outside the home. Not only would the cost be prohibitive, but also the cooking skills of the hostess could not be demonstrated. The custom of inviting people to a restaurant to celebrate an occasion and sharing the bill is usually viewed as very strange by Polish immigrants, especially if the host has in the past been invited to their home. Poles expect the same in return.

This does not mean that people in Poland do not go out to eat or share bills at restaurants. They do, but this is usually when they are on an excursion, on holiday, during a longer shopping expedition or to discuss a business deal - in other words, when they are unable to have a meal at home. Depending on their financial means, when Poles eat out they go fast food outlets, milk bars, cafés, bistros and restaurants.

Finally, unlike most people from English speaking countries, Poles consider surprise visits from friends quite normal. The Polish saying, 'Gość w dom, Bóg w dom. (A guest in the home is God in the home.) applies to invited guests and to surprise visitors alike. Also, impromptu get-togethers are common.

1. If you were to describe aspects of social life in your country to a Polish friend, what would you choose to describe and why?
2. Do you think there are any significant differences between social life of your country and that of Poland?

Things to Think About

1. (a) Is sport an important part of social life in Poland? Explain.
   (b) Is sport important in English speaking countries? Explain.
   (c) What impressions do you have of the role of sport in English speaking country where you live now?
   (d) Discuss your answers with the rest of the class.
2. Below is a questionnaire on behaviour at parties. First complete the questions yourself by entering 'yes' or 'no' in the column for Poland, then ask someone from an English speaking country to do likewise in the next column. Write the name of the English speaking country at the top of the last column.

Party customs	Poland	
1. Guests should always arrive on time.		
2. Guests often bring flowers for the hostess.		
3. Guests often bring drinks to a party.		
4. Guests often bring food to a party.		
5. Talking to people is an important part of the party.		
6. Talking about social, political and economic issues is acceptable at most parties.		
7. It is important to have a lot of food at a party.		
8. Children often accompany their parents to parties.		
9. People often dance at parties.		
10. Guests try to avoid being the first to arrive or the last to leave.		

3. (a) How is Christmas celebrated in the English speaking country in which you reside now?
   (b) Discuss with an English speaking friend the importance of Christmas.
   (c) What similarities and what differences are there in the way Christmas is observed in an English speaking country and in Poland?

Going Out for Entertainment

The local café is as much of an institution in Poland as the local pub in some English speaking countries. Even small towns and larger villages have cafés, and in the cities there are hundreds of them. They are always well patronised, the reason being that local cafés are ideal spots for meeting friends and to stop at for a while during long walks. They also have the right atmosphere to entertain friends, the privacy to discuss business and the convenience simply to gossip for a while over an espresso coffee or a glass of wine and a piece of cake. For retired people, spending a few hours at a café over a cup of coffee watching other people is probably better entertainment than watching television. When Poles go out to spend some time with friends, especially when they date or meet informally, they prefer to go to a café than a restaurant. They either stay there for the whole evening or proceed to other places.

Most young people in Poland enjoy similar forms of entertainment as their peers in English speaking countries. These include popular music concerts, discos, movies, sporting events—soccer being by far the most popular sport in Poland—and attractions available in the city or local centre. People with children, as elsewhere, tend to go out less, especially if they do not have parents or in-laws to look after the children. They tend to go for walks in local parks or visit other people with children.

All Poles, young and old, enjoy the theatre and concerts of popular and classical music. Many Polish immigrants and visitors to Australia, New Zealand, Canada and the United States complain about the lack of the more sophisticated forms of entertainment, such as theatrical performances of classical and modern plays and cabaret. These are all very popular in Poland and were until recently relatively inexpensive, as most companies were heavily subsidised by the government.

It is interesting that those who complain most about the lack of 'culture' in their adopted country, live mostly in large cities which offer a great variety of all manner of entertainment. There seem to be several reasons for this. First, newly arrived immigrants often do not have time or money for good entertainment, and they often do not realise that some entertainment may be inexpensive and even free of charge. Second, the language barrier prevents most Poles from regularly reading entertainment guides and art review columns in newspapers as they used to do in Poland. Lack of language competency also does not allow them to appreciate performances in English. Third, there are some forms of entertainment available in English speaking countries, particularly in the United States, which are not so popular and are sometimes virtually unknown in Poland. Poles may therefore have difficulty in appreciating them. It seems that encouragement to go out and try new types of entertainment is what most people need in order to discover that they can have as much fun going out in their newly adopted country as they had in Poland.

Things to Think About

1. How important do you think is the coffee shop in the social life of English speaking countries? Ask several people for their opinions. Are there any differences in the answers given by people of different ages or from different countries? How do these answers differ?

2. From the entertainment guide in your favourite English language newspaper, list all forms of entertainment advertised or reviewed in the entertainment guide, and then answer the following questions:
   (a) Are all the types of entertainment you have listed available in Poland?
   (b) Are any of these entertainments free? Which ones are they?
   (c) Which form of entertainment seems to be most popular?
   (d) Which of the listed forms of entertainment do you enjoy the most?
   (e) Have you been to any type of entertainment since your arrival in Australia? Why/why not?

3. Use the entertainment guide to find a performance you would like to see.
   (a) Find a review of this performance. What aspects of the performance does the review mention? What criticisms does it make?
   (b) Go and see the performance for yourself. Do you agree with the review? Explain.
   (c) Write a brief review of the performance yourself and present it to the class.

CHAPTER SIX

INTERACTING IN SOCIETY

Most language teaching textbooks place emphasis on language as the main means of communicating, but what they often do not deal with adequately is the cultural context. Differences in cultural backgrounds can lead to misunderstandings, which occur not only because of language incompetency, but also because different assumptions are made as to what are appropriate ways of communicating. Thus, when a Pole greets an Australian, each may expect a different response to the one given by the other person. Both, for instance, might begin by saying 'Hi!' and 'How are you today?', but when the Pole goes into a detailed description of his state of health, the Australian will probably think it strange, because 'How are you?' is not intended as a question, but is merely a part of the greeting. Different ways of showing respect and social distance further compound the problem (see pp. 45ff and 76–77).

As a result, social interactions are probably the most difficult for Polish learners to master because they have to overcome linguistic as well as cultural differences. Polish tends to be more direct, so that whenever Poles translate something from Polish directly into English—which is what many learners do until they are more competent in English—they often sound brusque and impolite, even though that is not their intention.

Socialising

Greetings

The way Poles greet others depends mainly on how well they know each other and, if they are not family or close friends, on their social status. Family and close friends are greeted informally, but, different greetings are used for more formal social contacts and for official and professional contacts. Equivalents of English greetings 'Hi' and 'Hello' (*Hej! Cześć! Serwus! Witaj!*) are reserved for good friends and family and are rarely, if ever, used when greeting strangers, especially if they are older or enjoy a higher social status. *Hej, Cześć!, Serwus!* or *Witaj!* would be considered impolite if used in an official situation.

Strangers in a professional situation are greeted with *Dzień dobry!*, (Good day) and *Dobry wieczór!* (Good evening). There are also a number of greetings which can be used in situations that are even more formal. There are: *Moje uszanowanie!* (My respects) and *Całuję rączki!* (I'm kissing your hands), a phrase used by men which either replaces or accompanies a kiss on a woman's hand. Official and professional greetings may be quite elaborate. These include, *Niech wolno mi będzie powitać szanownych gości* (Allow me to greet the respected guests), *Mam zaszczyt powitać gości* (I have the honour of greeting the guests) and *Witam z ogromną radością* (I am greeting with great joy).

The Polish phrase *Jak się masz?* literally translated means 'How are you?'. However, it is almost never used merely as a greeting. In Polish, the phrases *Jak się masz?, Co słychać?* (What's been happening?) and *Co u ciebie?* (How have you been doing?) are considered genuine questions and would not normally be asked of people one does not know very well, because asking such private questions of strangers would be considered intrusive. These questions are, however, appropriate to ask relatives and close friends.

Another characteristic feature of Polish greetings is physical contact. English speakers tend to shake hands only when they are introduced for the first time or on official occasions; and women kiss each other and men kiss women on the cheek. Poles, on the other hand, do this each time they meet. Men shake hands with other men and only sometimes with women. Men usually kiss women's hands in greeting, which is not liked by all women, especially younger ones, but most accept the custom and even expect it when they are older. The fact that most women from English speaking countries prefer to shake hands, can lead to confusion when greeting Poles, as Klos Sokol (1994) points out:

> I've often made the mistake of gripping a gentleman's hand with the intention of giving a firm shake and ended up with a clumsy twist in mid-air as he wrestled a kiss onto the back of my hand. (p. 14)

Poles of both sexes often embrace each other, kiss each other on the cheeks and are generally much more physical when greeting each other than are people from most English speaking countries.

---

1. How do the greetings in English speaking cultures differ from those in Poland?
2. How do you think your Polish students might feel about the greeting customs observed in English speaking cultures?
3. If you are a woman, how do you think you would react if a Polish male friend kissed your hand in greeting?
4. How do you think you would feel if a male student did likewise?

Things to Think About

1. Discuss with the rest of your class the different ways people greet each other in different cultures. What do these greetings have in common?
2. Compare Polish greeting customs with those of English speaking cultures. Make a list of all the phrases you can think of in both languages and the gestures that accompany them. What similarities and what differences are there?

Introductions

In Polish context only children and teenagers are introduced to each other informally, using first names and second person singular of the verb. Adults, on the other hand, are addressed formally, irrespective of whether introductions are made during formal occasions or at casual functions. Adults use both first and family names, and especially in very formal situations *pan, pani, państwo* or professional titles are used. Poles often pay less attention to the first names—even though in introductions first names are often mentioned first—because when people are addressed later, it is their family name and professional title that will need to be remembered. This may be one reason why they have problems remembering the first names of all their English speaking friends.

The most important rule on introductions in Polish culture is that a man should always be introduced to a woman, a person of lower social status to a person of a higher status and a younger person to an older person. After they have been introduced, people usually shake hands and men sometimes kiss the women's hand.

Here are three forms of Polish introductions:

1. *Informal introduction within families and between children and teenagers.* First names are used, thus:

   Marysia—Jurek
   (Mary—George)

2. *Informal introduction between adults.* The man is introduced to the woman; first and family names are used thus:

   Zbigniew Gryka—Janina Gumkowska
   (Zbigniew Gryka [male]—Janina Gumkowska [female])

3. *Official or professional introduction.* The person of lower status is introduced to the person of higher status irrespective of sex; family names, first names and titles are used thus:

   Panie profesorze, Maria Nawrocka—profesor Andrzej Sadza
   (Professor, this is Maria Nawrocka—professor Andrzej Sadza)

Things to Think About

1. How would you introduce the following people to each other? Role play the introductions, not forgetting the body language!
   (i) Paul Carter, 26 years old, and Jenny Thomas, 28 years old (at a party).
   (ii) David Hill, 37 years old, a new employee, to his workmates.
   (iii) Alex Thorne, a post-graduate student, to Pauline Wolfe, a professor (at a conference).

> (iv) Edward Joyce, an accountant, to Ruth Howe, a personnel manager (at a business meeting).
>
> (v) Jane Simpson, a friend of your own age, to your parents.
>
> **2.** (a) How do you feel about using your English teacher's first name in and outside the classroom?
>
> (b) Would you feel comfortable introducing your English teacher to your friends using the teacher's first name only?
>
> (c) How do you feel when much younger people than yourself address you by your first name?

Social Conversation

There is a significant difference between Polish and English speaking cultures in what are considered to be appropriate conversation topics. For most Poles, a social conversation at a party provides an ideal opportunity for a serious discussion on controversial topics. Many English speakers, however, tend to feel uncomfortable debating controversial issues in this setting. This difference can result in Polish and English speaking people making negative impressions on each other, without intending to do so, which can lead to the formation of mutually negative impressions.

Polish parties are often around a dinner table, with men and women seated alternately. Each man is expected to serve the woman sitting on his left and to talk mainly to her. The conversation is likely to revolve around the current political situation, the activities of mutual acquaintances and the party itself. After the meal is over, people either remain at the table or they move away, but in either case the conversation will become more involved, with topics such as politics and social issues being discussed. The conversation is usually loud and animated, with people trying to convince each other about their own points of view, and seldom agreeing with each other.

Many English speakers witnessing such a conversation may think that Poles are quarrelsome, rude and opinionated, and fail to realise that Polish people enjoy such conversations. In fact, at a larger party, where several conversations may be in progress, the liveliest one will attract most people, many of whom will join in the discussion. Poles often find conversations about personal interests and activities of the speakers mundane and irrelevant.

As well as lively conversations, Poles also enjoy telling political and other types of jokes, usually towards the end of the party. A good joke teller is always considered an asset at a party. A successful Polish party is therefore one at which conversations are rapid and amusing, subjects are debated and good jokes are told.

Talking Distance

The comfortable talking distance in Polish and English speaking cultures is different. As Klos Sokol (1994) points out, people from English speaking countries may be:

. . . unnerved by the Polish casual conversation zone, which seems to be about two to four inches smaller than the American one—a short distance but enough to feel that creepy in-your-face effect which makes you pull back to the comfort zone. Which of course makes the other person lean in closer and has you feeling like conversational pray. (p. 62)

People brought up in English speaking cultures tend to avoid physical contact, while Poles, who are not so reserved about touching others, tend to adjust the talking distance according to the subject of the conversation or how well they know the other person. Thus, while the conversation remains neutral, the talking distance between the two speakers is likely to be comfortable for both people. However, if the conversation becomes emotional, there is a disagreement or a point is to be made, a Polish person will move closer to the other person. If the other person moves away, the Pole will follow and might even grab the other person to stop them moving. Polish people will often do that, for according to them, how can anyone be really involved in a conversation at a distance!

Things to Think About

1. Make up a list of subjects you would consider suitable for a conversation at a Polish party and then ask two or three of your English speaking friends to list subjects of conversation they would consider appropriate for one of their parties.
   (a) Compare the two lists.
   (b) Ask your friends if they would consider any of the subjects on your list which do not appear on theirs as appropriate for a party. If they do not find any suitable topics, ask them why this is so?
   (c) Discuss your findings with the rest of your class.
2. (a) Is sport an important topic of conversation for any particular group of people? If so, which group?
   (b) Ask an English speaking friend their opinion on this matter. How similar is your attitude to your friend's?

Leave Taking

One difference that non-Poles notice immediately about leave taking in the Polish culture is the reluctance to leave a good party, especially when no time has been specified for its conclusion. When they are having a good time, Poles tend to stay very late, often until well after midnight. As Klos Sokol (1994) comments:

Guests are not allowed to leave, so any inclination toward the door elicits protests . . . You stay a little longer but feel almost guilty trying to take leave again when they express their disappointment, *'Nie, jeszcze jest wcześnie!'* (No, it's still early!). In a last ditch effort to convince you to down one more drink, Polish hosts will announce, *'Strzemiennego'* (for the stirrups). When their third protest rolls around, it may not mean that they really want you to stay; they are just following the rules of gracious hosting. (p. 18)

When guests do eventually leave, most of them go at roughly the same time, but it is not considered good manners if all guests leave together. If it is very late, only symbolic intervals of a few minutes are left between individual departures. Every guest tells the host how enjoyable the party was and how delicious the food was. Not to do this is considered impolite.

Things to Think About

Observe how English speakers take leave of each other by listening to people around you, to films and television dramas and by reading modern novels and short stories.
(a) Find examples of what the following types of people say:
    (i) Colleagues leaving work.
    (ii) A secretary and manager leaving work.
    (iii) Two school students going home after school.
    (iv) A person leaving a friend's place after a quick visit.
    (v) A person leaving a friend's place after a dinner party.
    (vi) A student and the teacher after class.
    (vii) Two elderly friends leaving a café.
    (viii) An elderly person and a much younger acquaintance after a party
(b) Are there any differences with what Poles would say in the same situations?

Agreeing, Disagreeing and Expressing Opinions

There are major differences in the way opinions are expressed in Polish and in English. Other than the language, it is the avoidance of confrontation and not wanting to be thought opinionated that differentiates English speakers from Poles. It follows that learning to argue in English in an acceptable way will present serious difficulties to Poles, particularly because different communication strategies are used in the two languages to express opinions and disagreements.

Expressing Opinions and Disagreements

Poles tend to be direct when they express opinions or when they disagree, since an argument is not only considered a good way of exchanging ideas, but also an enjoyable form of conversation. Consequently, the primary aim of many Poles when expressing an opinion is to state it in such a manner that will be difficult to refute it. So, if one is sure of what one is saying, openers such as *Jestem absolutnie pewna, że . . .* (I'm absolutely sure that . . .), *Nie mam najmniejszych wątpliwości . . .* (I have no doubts whatsoever . . .), *Głowę daję, że . . .* (I'll risk my head that . . .) and *Każdy głupi wie, że . . .* (Every fool knows that . . .) are totally acceptable, although the last two would not be used in formal situations. If one is not certain, conditional or milder openers can be used, for example, *Chyba . . .* , *Przypuszczalnie* (Probably . . .), *Jestem prawie pewien . . .* (I'm almost sure), *Myślę, że . . .* (I think that . . .) and *Mam wrażenie, że . . .* (I am under the impression that . . .).

The main difference between Polish and English usage is that while some of the more temperate openers are equally suitable in both languages, the proposition that follows will be expressed directly in Polish but is often modified in English. Thus, while a Polish person would say:

> *Mam wrażenie, że ten obraz jest bezwartościowy.*
> (I'm under the impression that this painting is worthless.)

in English this would be said much more diplomatically, thus:

> I don't really think this is a very good painting.

In Polish if people do not agree about a point, they do not 'beat about the bush'. If they disagree, they will say so without mincing their words, although in formal or official situations disagreement may be expressed slightly more politely. Thus Poles do not hesitate to use a straightforward *Nie!* (No!) to show that they disagree during an informal argument, or such phrases as *Wcale nie!* (No way!), *Nic podobnego!* (Nothing of the sort!), *Nieprawda!* (Not true!), *Mylisz się!* (You're wrong!), *To jest bez sensu!* (There's no sense in it!), *Nie zgadzam się!* (I disagree!) and *Chyba zwariowałeś!* (You must be mad!) even with strangers. However, when talking with strangers, the titles *pan, pani* and *państwo* are added where appropriate. Except for the last one, the above phrases can be used even in very formal situations by simply adding appropriate titles and/or softeners. For example:

> *Pozwolę sobie zauważyć, że pani profesor myli się.*
> (Let me note that you are wrong, professor.)

Here the message 'You are wrong!' remains, but it is preceded by the polite opener 'Let me note . . .' and the title 'professor' to make it acceptable in a formal situation.

Debating

Many Poles tend to transfer their Polish customs of debating into English without any modifications. Consequently, they may seem impolite and opinionated. This does not mean that Poles are unwilling to accept other's opinion; rather, they feel that the other person needs to be told in no uncertain terms that they are wrong. Here is one example of how an English speaking person may feel uncomfortable in a situation such as that:

Two Polish friends were having a disagreement over the definition of a word in

Polish. Their spat was making me uneasy. They consulted a dictionary but then quarrelled over the word's implications. When I tried to change the subject, they ignored me. Finally, the conversation eased into another topic as if nothing had happened. The only person rattled by the little battle was me—the American. (Klos Sokol 1994, p. 66)

For most Poles, debating is not just a way of solving problems or a competition enjoyed by few. Rather, it is an acceptable way of spending time pleasantly while learning something about an issue. While both cultures share the general aim of a debate—the presentation of arguments for and against a point of view in order to reach a conclusion—only those English speakers who debate professionally or as a hobby attach much importance to the debating skill itself and to the question of who the winner is. Because English speakers tend to avoid imposing their views on others or hurting others' feelings, they tend not to debate socially. Instead, the art of debating is usually cultivated either as a professional tool for solving problems in settings such as the parliament, local councils or business, or it is put into the context of a competition. If a controversial topic is brought into normal social interaction, English speakers often remain silent until the speaker has finished and then attempt to change the subject, laugh it off or even walk away.

Not so with Poles. For them debating serious, political, social or personal issues is one of the favourite social activities. So much so that to liven up a party, people will sometimes make slightly provocative statements with the sole purpose of starting a debate.

This inclination to discuss serious subjects was further developed during the Communist rule when genuine discussion was largely absent from public life. Instead, most meaningful discussions on serious issues took place in private settings. It is not surprising then that Polish society often appeared to foreigners to be an enormous debating club; almost every private gathering of Poles included discussions, often heated ones, of serious social, political and moral issues. In the absence of good examples of debating in the media and public life, these discussions often became a little disorderly and people often found it hard to give up their point of view. Thus the saying that there are as many opinions as there are Poles was often true.

When a controversial subject is brought up, it will often be picked up by those present. Anyone who disagrees will usually wait for the speaker to finish and then clearly state their argument and wait for a refutation. A debate such as this can go on for hours, the participants trying to persuade each other by arguing each point in turn. Other listeners often join in the argument, each trying to gain the upper hand as the debate heats up. The point is not so much to win as to defend one's point of view in a skilful, witty manner, which will be appreciated by those taking part as well as those listening. A spirited debate leaves Poles feeling satisfied, even if they do not win.

1. How would you help your Polish students to seem less aggressive when expressing their opinions?
2. Many Poles find the topics of conversation touched on in English conversations to be trivial.
   (a) Should an English teacher try to counter this impression?
   (b) If so, how can this be done?

Things to Think About

1. Marysia Sobieska, a new immigrant from Poland, thinks she has discovered a good business opportunity. She spoke about it to Jane Goodall, an English speaking friend, as follows:

   MS: Jane, I've just discovered an excellent way of making some money. All I have to do is address envelopes and from that I can make up to $400 a week. It's fantastic, isn't it?

   JG: How did you find out about it?

   MS: Oh, I saw an advertisement in the Sunday paper.

   JG: Some of these advertisements are hoaxes, you know.

   MS: Oh yes, I know Jane, but this one said it was 'a respectable overseas company'. Don't you think it is a good idea to send them $20 and get into business?

   JG: Are you sure it's not a rip-off?

   MS: I am sure it won't take me more than three hours a day and Jan and I could do with a little extra money now that we bought a house. So, what do you think, Jane? Is it good or not?

   JG: Well, I'd think twice before I sent them $20.

   MS: So you don't think this is a good idea?

   JG: Oh, I didn't say that. It's just that you've got to be careful with those ads.

   MS: Oh, Jane, why won't you ever say 'yes' or 'no'. Come on, tell me, do you think that this is a good idea, or don't you?

   JG: Well, I suppose you know what you are doing. Incidentally, I heard you did well in your computer course. Congratulations!

   (a) How do you think Marysia feels about the outcome of the conversation?
   (b) Why do you think Jane avoided any strong expression of opinion?
   (c) What does Jane think of the opportunity? Study the conversation again and explain what Jane actually meant by each of her comments.
2. Write down five controversial statements and read them to another person. In pairs, roleplay different ways of disagreeing with these statements.

Expressing Emotions and Feelings

Most people brought up in English speaking cultures tend to be more reserved in expressing their feelings than Poles. While both cultures consider violent expressions of emotion to be undesirable, they differ significantly in the way positive feelings are expressed.

Poles will readily express such feelings as love, friendship, compassion and appreciation, both verbally and physically. Kissing, hugging, patting on the back and holding hands is totally acceptable and even expected in many situations. Family members and close friends often kiss or hug each other. Even people who are not close, such as friends from work or neighbours, will pat each other on the back or shake hands. This may make people from English speaking countries uncomfortable, even though these behaviours are quite natural to Poles.

There are also considerable differences between the two cultures when it comes to expressing feelings verbally, not only in the choice of words but also whether or not to talk about feelings in the first place. On the whole, English speakers seem to be less emotional and hence more polite than Poles when talking about their emotions. They seem to talk about their negative feelings sooner and in a more restrained manner in an attempt to solve problems before they become explosive. Poles, on the other hand, will often deal with their negative feelings later and impulsively, when tension is high. As a result, anger, dissatisfaction and ill feeling are usually expressed in more direct terms and consequently sound more forceful and emotional. Here are a few examples of angry reactions:

Bezczelność!
(Impertinence!)

(said after an improper request has been made);

Rany boskie!
(For God's sake!)

(said after realising that the other person has made a mess of something);

Nie znoszę pańskich głupich dowcipów!
(I can't bear your stupid jokes!)

(a reaction to an annoying joke).

Ill feeling towards a person or object will also be expressed directly, thus:

Jan, jest okropny!
(Jan is horrible!)

An unpleasant surprise may be expressed in an equally straightforward manner, thus:

Naprawdę?
(Really?)

Oszalałeś?

(Are you mad?)

Jak to?!
(What do you mean?)

While formal situations require some moderation, even phrases such as *Jestem niezadowolony* (I am dissatisfied), *Jan mnie uraził* (Jan offended me), *Jan mnie irytuje* (Jan irritates me) or *Pan mówi poważnie?* (Are you serious about what you are saying?) might sound too direct to a native English speaker.

Positive feelings and emotions are also expressed differently in Polish and in English. While the expressions used are similar, usage is not. First, most English speakers tend to be reserved when talking about intimate feelings in public. Polish, on the other hand, distinguishes between the familiar and unfamiliar forms of address, which are an immediate indicator of the degree of intimacy between people. Second, Poles rarely hesitate to use words such as 'like', 'adore' and 'love'. Last, but not least, Polish has an extremely well developed range of diminutive forms, which are used to express intimate feelings, both in speech and in writing.

If some deeper emotions are touched, be it the feeling of patriotism, pride or compassion, a Pole will often act almost immediately and on impulse. If someone makes unpleasant remarks about Poland, any Poles present will most probably not only feel offended, but will storm out and refuse to return.

Poles may at times feel that their English speaking friends are calculating and lacking in strong emotions and warmth. For example, English speakers tend not to hug a person to congratulate them or even shake their hand, though they may say 'Well done'. On the other hand, the behaviour of Polish people may be interpreted by English speakers as irrational and rude. To them, Poles seem to act rashly, without giving issues proper consideration.

---

1. To what extent do you think your culture encourages open expression of feelings? Give examples.
2. How would you explain these attitudes to a group of Polish students?

Things to Think About

Below is a questionnaire on how emotions are expressed in Polish and in English. Complete the questionnaire yourself by ticking the answers that apply to you. (You can tick more than one answer for any one question.) Ask an English speaking friend to do likewise.

Situation	Polish	English
1. You are at the airport meeting a very close friend whom you have not seen for over 10 years. He has just emerged from customs control with his wife whom you have not met and his four-year old son. Would you: (a) kiss him? (b) embrace him? (c) shake hands with him? (d) tell him that you missed him? (e) kiss his wife? (f) embrace his wife? (g) shake hands with his wife? (h) kiss his son? (i) embrace his son? (j) shake hands with his son?		
2. Your friend and his family are planning to spend a fortnight with you and the rest of the two-month holiday travelling. You have a family of your own and a two-bedroom house with a study. You would have to turn the study into a temporary bedroom to accommodate your friends. Would you: (a) invite them to stay at your house? (b) if they declined, insist that they stay in your house during the two weeks? (c) arrange a hotel/motel for them?		
3. You find out that your friend's mother, whom you knew well, died recently. Would you: (a) offer formal condolences? (b) express your grief personally? (c) embrace your friend to express sympathy? (d) ask about the circumstances of her death? (e) talk with your friend about his mother?		
4. Your friend's son tripped and hurt himself. Would you: (a) do nothing—call the parents? (b) show sympathy, then call the parents? (c) pick him up and take him to his parents? (d) embrace him, give him a sweet, then tell the parents what happened? (e) tell him that big boys don't cry?		
5. Your friends are leaving after a very pleasant two-week visit. You have spent a lot of time together and have all become very friendly. When parting would you: (a) kiss and embrace your friend?		

Situation	Polish	English
(b) kiss and embrace your friend's wife?		
(c) kiss and embrace your friend's son?		
6. You are at a cocktail party. You have just joined a group of five people, including John Black, a good friend of yours, and Ian McGregor, who you detest. Would you:		
(a) talk exclusively to John?		
(b) talk to everyone in the group?		
(c) pointedly ignore Ian McGregor?		
(d) be impolite to Ian, if he talks to you?		
7. A colleague at work has just behaved in a way that annoys you. Would you:		
(a) politely tell the person at once that you do not like their behaviour?		
(b) wait and see whether the person does it again and then react?		
(c) wait until you cannot bear it any longer? then tell the person what you think of them?		
(d) say nothing?		

(a) Are there any major differences in the two responses? What are they?

(b) Discuss your findings with the rest of your class.

Paying Compliments

Polish culture makes a clear distinction between compliments in social situations and compliments in all other situations. It is customary for men and women to exchange compliments at informal social gatherings and the guests to compliment the host or hostess at the conclusion of a function. This is, in fact, the only situation in which compliments are paid freely to others irrespective of whether they deserve them or not. In other words, when Poles meet to enjoy themselves socially, the main reason for complimenting others is to initiate conversation, to create a festive atmosphere and to show appreciation of the host or hostess for their effort.

A man may complement a woman on her appearance and may accompany that with subtle sexual connotations, but this is not predominant. The woman usually thanks the man for the compliment, and she may give him one in return, usually by referring to his conduct rather than his looks. It is customary to flirt. Here are some examples of typical compliments made by men:

Świetnie wygląz!
(You look extremely well!)

Pięknie wyglądasz w tej sukience!
(You look beautiful in this dress!)

Cudownie pani tańczy.
(You're a wonderful dancer, madam.)

Ma pani piękne oczy.
(You've got beautiful eyes, madam.)

Women accept such compliments by giving the non-committal answer thus:

Bardzo mi miło.
(It's nice of you.)

or by immediately returning the compliment, thus:

Jesteś bardzo miły.
(You are very nice.)

Jesteś wspaniały!
(You are wonderful!)

Jest pan bardzo uprzejmy.
(You are very polite, sir.)

In response, men will usually refute the compliment thus:

Przesadzasz.
(You're exaggerating.)

People of English speaking background may fail to understand that such compliments are an accepted part of informal social interaction and are not in general perceived as having patronising, sexual or sexist overtones.

Completely different compliments are used when people are being complemented for specific reasons. It seems to many Poles that English speakers are fulsome about everyday events and objects. They seem to use elaborate language to talk about things that really deserve no more than a mention. For example, an ugly piece of furniture is described as 'interesting' and an average vase as 'charming'. By comparison, Poles are much more reserved in using elaborate language because other than at a social gathering, they do not believe in giving praise where it is not deserved. Thus, while an ugly piece of furniture would not be actually called ugly, most Poles would either say nothing or they would acknowledge the object with a neutral comment. Poles may seem, therefore, rude to English speakers because of what they do not say, since they often fail to say anything positive when expected. English speakers, on the other hand, will often be perceived by Poles as drowning genuine compliments in a flood of superfluous positive comments.

How would you incorporate the different ways of complimenting in Polish and English speaking cultures into your teaching?

Things to Think About

1. English speakers who know little about Polish culture often perceive Polish men as sexist because of the way they give compliments. Based on what you understand about the cultures in English speaking countries, explain why English speakers may have this perception of the Poles.

2. What would you say in the following situations?

   (a) You are a female teacher. A fellow female teacher has just come to work wearing a new dress.

   (b) You are a male teacher. A fellow female teacher has just come to work wearing a new suit.

   (c) A friend of yours is singing in a choir. You go to hear her sing, but really do not enjoy the concert.

   (d) A friend of yours has just moved into a new flat.

   (e) You are at a party, talking to a woman you have just met.

Requesting and Refusing

When speaking English, Poles often sound abrupt when they ask for help, permission or service, or when they refuse to do something. This is mainly due to the fact that the Polish language uses different means from English not only to formulate requests, but also to make them polite. It is also due to cultural differences in the use of the familiar forms in addressing people, which lead learners to false generalisations regarding the use of formal and familiar forms of request.

The Polish language reserves the use of the first name and second person of the verb for children and for family and close friends. As a result, in informal situations requests and refusals do not need to be made in a polite manner, for children, family and close friends can be asked or refused directly. People who are addressed formally with the titles *pan, pani* or *państwo* and third person of the verb are asked or refused very politely, especially if they are strangers. However, people who have higher status—including employers and older people—are addressed more politely than people of lower status, including young people and employees.

While most requests implicitly contain a command or directive, the use of the imperative in English is very restricted for reasons of politeness. In fact, every effort is made to avoid using it and, consequently indirect requests, often including the use of the conditional, are the preferred form. By contrast, in Polish the imperative and various constructions with the infinitive are used mostly to request or to order and, wherever applicable, first names, nicknames and their diminutives are used to make the message sound friendly and polite. The two following situations illustrate this.

A person with a pack of cigarettes at an informal barbecue could be asked:

Daj Józiu papieroska jeśli masz.
(Pass me a cigarette, Joe, if you have one.)

At a formal dinner party, however, a person would be asked to pass the salt in the following way:

Czy mógłby pan proszę podać sól?
(Could you please pass me the salt, sir?)

In the first situation the imperative is used, but the second degree diminutive of the name *Józef* (*Józiu*) is used to stress the intimacy of the relationship. The use of the imperative, if translated directly into English, is likely to sound demanding. English speakers in the same situation tend to use modals or question tags to soften the message.

In the second, more formal situation, the request is made in a way that is similar to English, except for the use of 'sir'. However, requests such as these are used only in formal situations, in which the person making the request is in a subordinate position in relation to the person being addressed. If the person making the request is in a superior position, even polite requests will sound abrupt if they are translated directly into English. Here are some examples of requests which could be made by a person in authority, in this case a university lecturer requesting the students to sit down:

Proszę siadać!
(Please, be seated!)

Niech wszyscy siadają!
(All will sit down!)

Państwo usiądą!
(You will sit down, ladies and gentlemen!)

Państwo będą uprzejmi usiąść.
(You will kindly sit, ladies and gentlemen.)

The examples above are arranged from the least to most polite. Despite the words *państwo*—which is less courteous than 'ladies and gentlemen' and has no exact equivalent in English—and 'kindly', the last example sounds abrupt in English. If the same message was intended as a command or order, just one word, *Siadać!* (the infinitive of 'to sit') uttered sharply would suffice.

Requests and demands are refused similarly, with a plain *nie!* (no!) or by equally abrupt refusals such as:

Nie mogę.
(I can't!)

Ani mi się śni!
(I wouldn't even dream about it!)

The same type of negative answers would be acceptable among family and friends, provided a diminutive of the first name or nickname is used to make the refusal sound friendly.

Sometimes Poles use patterns which are somewhat similar to English, such as:

Niestety, nie mogę.
(Unfortunately, I can't.)

Przykro mi, ale nie jestem w stanie tego zrobić.
(I'm sorry, but I am not in a position to do this.)

Niestety muszę państwu odmówić.
(Unfortunately, I have to refuse you.)

In the last example, the untranslatable word *państwo*, meaning 'you' makes the refusal polite. Unlike in English speaking cultures, in Polish such polite refusals would only be used in informal situations when someone is really going out of their way to soften the refusal and in neutral official situations, such as a conversation between a clerk and a customer in a government office.

Thus, in English speaking cultures it is correct to make requests and refuse in a polite manner. However, the way this is done differs considerably. The greatest difference concerns requests and refusals made by people in authority. An English speaker may find requests and refusals translated from Polish directly into English rather abrupt. Polish learners are therefore confronted with the task of suppressing the urge to be formal with relative strangers by calling almost everybody by their first name, and by using the second person of the verb when addressing them. They may come to the incorrect conclusion that Polish forms of communication used in the family and among close friends are appropriate for use across the board in English. Following Polish custom, they are likely to use direct rather than polite forms, which may lead to serious problems with their subordinates, who will consider them extremely rude.

Over-generalisation of cultural rules and transfer of rules from one culture to another are errors language learners often make.
(a) How would you teach your students about these common mistakes?
(b) How would you help those students who are making these errors to rectify them?

Things to Think About

1. Wanda Niedzielska is an outstanding specialist in industrial biochemistry. She was invited to Australia by a pharmaceutical company to head a team testing a new drug. The contract was initially for a year, with the possibility of extending it for three years if the results seemed promising. Wanda's first letters home were enthusiastic. She was impressed with the friendly atmosphere and in particular with the way she was welcomed and introduced to her new job and the team she was to work with. It is now six months since the start of her contract and it seems her impressions have changed drastically. Here is a part of a letter she recently sent her mother in Poland:

   . . . I must say that my initial impressions about working in Australia were quite exaggerated. It appears that the friendly attitudes I met here at the beginning are gone altogether—not so much in private contacts as at work. It seems that, after the initial enthusiasm, my employees have now changed completely—they seem unhappy to work with me, they are slow and lazy in doing what I ask them to do and do not show any involvement in developing proposals for the future. If it goes on like this, I will never be able to get an extension of the contract.

   (a) Based on your understanding of the differences in how requests and refusals are communicated in English and in Polish, what do you thing might be the explanation for Wanda's experience?
   (b) What advice would you give Wanda to help her solve the problem?

2. You have just written an English essay and you would like someone to check it for you. How would you ask the following people to do it for you:
   (i)   Your English speaking wife/husband.
   (ii)   Allan Smith, a colleague at work.
   (iii)   An elderly neighbour who is a university professor.
   (iv)   Your English teacher.
   (v)   A fellow student from your language class.
   (vi)   An elderly neighbour who is a builder.
   (vii) Your girlfriend/boyfriend.
   (viii) A postgraduate student from the English Department, whom you do not know very well.
   (ix)   Angela Lockwood, your mother-in-law.
   (x)   Your 11 year old son, who is a native speaker of English.

3. You are flying to Europe and an elderly friend of yours has asked you to take a 2 kilogram parcel to someone in London. You will have too much of your own luggage, so you have to refuse.
   (a) Roleplay with a partner five different ways of refusing the elderly friend.

    (b) Classify each refusal according to how negative it is.
4. In pairs. chose one of the following situations and develop a dialogue around it. Present your dialogue to the class.
    (a) Your friend Mary has agreed to give you a lift to town in her car. You have just started on your journey when you remember that you have left your wallet at home and you must go back and get it.
    (b) Tony, one of your fellow students, has agreed to give you a lift home in his car. At the very start of your journey you realise that the car is unsafe and Tony is a very reckless driver. You ask him politely to stop but this has no effect, so you have to firmly demand that he stop.
    (c) You are a foreman in a carpenter's workshop. It is morning and you are setting your subordinates their tasks for the day. How would you ask the following people to do the tasks specified:
      (i) Larry Baxter to fix a squeaky table and six chairs before 3 o'clock, then help John Sweet.
      (ii) John Sweet to continue making shelves.
      (iii) Ian Laws to start a new job—making 24 chairs.
      (iv) Sue Wills to varnish all the shelves made yesterday by John.

Apologising

Apologies are made in a similar way in Polish as they are in English. In Polish, the degree of familiarity with the offended person influences to some extent the form of apology used, but the differences in the apologies are not so pronounced as when requests are made. Apologies are straightforward when they are made to intimate friends or family members. For example:

Przepraszam!
(I'm sorry!)

Strasznie mi głupio, że . . .
(It was very silly of me to . . .)

Wybacz!
(Forgive me!)

Nie gniewaj się!
(Don't be angry with me!)

In less intimate situations the apologies are more elaborate and include the titles *pan*, *pani* and *państwo*. For example:

Bardzo pana przepraszam!
(I'm very sorry, sir!)

Proszę mi wybaczyć.
(Please forgive me.)

Note that the infinitive is used to avoid using the second person of the verb or the imperative:

Strasznie mi przykro, że . . .
(I am terribly sorry that . . .)

In official and professional situations, as well as when there are big differences in social status, more formal or very elaborate apologies are expected. Not all apologies are readily translatable into English, especially when titles are used. For example:

Przepraszam pana, panie dyrektorze!
(I am sorry, Mr director!)

Ogromnie państwa przepraszam!
(I am exceedingly sorry, Mr and Mrs . . .)

Chciałbym przeprosić za . . .
(I'd like to apologise for . . .)

The reasons for and the frequency of apologies differ between Polish and English. Poles tend not to apologise for trifles, whether at home, to friends, in shops or in restaurants. For example, if a person steps on someone's toe, they will apologise whether they are Polish or from an English speaking country. However, if a person accidentally bumps into someone during a conversation, an apology may be expected by an English speaking person but not by a Pole. No apology is necessary in Polish if someone corrects or disagrees with another person, unless that person is the boss. While an employee would be expected to apologise to the boss for completing a job late, not many bosses would seriously consider apologising to their employees in everyday work encounters. If an apology is considered necessary, except for contacts with family and close friends Polish apologies tend to be flowery, or humble if it is being made to a superior.

The different forms of apologies described above are, admittedly, vague, for the appropriateness of apology is usually based on individual's judgment in both cultures. It seems that the easiest way for Polish immigrants to learn appropriate ways of apologising in English is simply to say 'I am sorry' more often.

'It's not the how but the when that's difficult.' Do you agree with this statement made by a teacher about the difficulties associated with a functional approach to language learning? Give reasons for your answer.

Things to Think About

1. (a) In English, which of the situations described below require an apology?
   (b) What would be the correct apology for each of these situations?
   (c) In pairs, roleplay each situation. The rest of the class is then to comment on the appropriateness of the dialogue.
      (i) You have to leave class early because of an urgent appointment.
      (ii) You arrive half an hour late to a dinner party.
      (iii) Your trolley bumps into another person's trolley in the supermarket.
      (iv) You forget to bring a book you had promised to lend to a friend.
      (v) You spill coffee over your professor's desk.
      (vi) You break a valuable vase belonging to a friend.

Offering, Accepting and Declining

Poles and people from English speaking countries offer, accept and decline gifts, services and favours in almost the same way. The main differences occur when celebrations are organised at which food is shared. This is connected specifically with the Polish concept of hospitality.

A long time ago, this Polish saying was coined: *Zastaw się, a postaw się* (Show off, even if you have to pawn something) to describe the custom of organising lavish parties even if the hosts could not really afford them. This was true not only of the wealthy gentry, but also among simple folk, who readily spent a whole year's earnings on a christening or a wedding. Even today many Poles follow the same tradition when it comes to celebrations, at which food is usually plentiful and rich.

It is assumed in Polish culture that the host should show hospitality by providing plenty of food and drink for the guests. Guests, in turn, are expected to show their appreciation by consuming the food and drink. Thus, Polish hosts tend to be very pleasantly but firmly insistent that their guests eat and drink what is being served and, unlike most hosts of English speaking backgrounds, they do not take 'no' for an answer. This was confirmed by the observations of one American, who described her experience as follows:

> As a guest in the Polish household, it's difficult to go wrong with politeness. If you are offered something to eat or drink, it's polite to say '*tak, proszę,*' for 'yes, please,' since the successful guest is the guest who consumes. It's also polite to turn the offer down with '*dziękuję*' to mean 'no thanks,' since that provides the person with the opportunity to host to the hilt and reoffer until you say 'yes.' Stuffing yourself silly is proper behaviour. And all hosts assume you are there to behave properly. When you've reached your limit, it takes a series of firm *dziękuję's* (three minimum) to stop the process. (Klos Sokol 1994, p. 17)

As a result, most English speakers visiting Polish homes eat plenty because their

Polish hosts insist that they continue eating, despite repeated polite refusals. By contrast, most Poles living in English speaking countries think that the locals are misers when it comes to inviting people and sharing food with them. Poles are surprised when they find out that their English speaking hosts happily accept and sometimes even expect their guests to bring food and drinks with them, and that after the initial invitation to eat and drink they seldom invite people to have seconds. Poles, who are used to having food and drinks offered to them repeatedly, usually serve themselves the first time round less than they intend to eat, and as a result, often leave such parties hungry.

Things to Think About

Below is a questionnaire on attitudes about parties. Give the questionnaire to an English speaking friend and a Polish friend to do. They are to write 'yes' or 'no' in the appropriate columns.

Question	English	Polish
1. You are often expected to bring food to a party.		
2. You are usually expected to bring drinks.		
3. The hosts supply all the food at a party.		
4. The hosts supply all the drinks for the party.		
5. Guests help themselves to food and drinks as they please.		
6. Guests should be repeatedly encouraged to eat and drink.		
7. If guests say that they do not want any more to eat, it would be impolite to encourage them to have some more.		
8. If guests say that they do not want any more to drink, they should be encouraged to change their mind.		

(a) Compare the results in the two columns.
(b) Are the answers consistent with other aspects of the cultures of English speaking countries?

CHAPTER SEVEN

TEACHING AND LEARNING IN POLAND

The Education System in Poland

The Polish education system is firmly based on the traditional view that acquiring a prescribed body of knowledge and skills is a precondition for choice and creativity. The system also places greater emphasis on academic achievement at both primary level and in high school than do the educational systems in most English speaking countries, and much less emphasis on preparing students for the practicalities of everyday life.

Primary School Level

Children enter primary school when they are seven years old. The primary level includes grades 1 to 8, is considered the best place to teach reading, writing and arithmetic, which are taught mostly by rote in years 1 to 4. Years 5 to 8 are devoted to further development in these areas, as well as to teaching basic facts in subjects such as geography, history, biology, physics and at least one foreign language. Children are required to repeat grades if they fail in any of the important subjects, such as Polish and mathematics. As a result, pressure is put on the children to achieve. School attendance is compulsory up to the age of sixteen.

While there is some room for creativity, discovery and games in Polish primary schools, the volume of material to be learned and consequently the amount of homework assigned from grade 3 onwards is significantly greater than in United States, Australian, British or Canadian primary schools. Thus, while English speaking children tend to treat the first few grades as an extension of kindergarten and therefore usually enjoy primary school, Polish children associate school more with duty and work and less with pleasure.

High School Level

High school is a continuation of the same process. The most obvious difference between Polish and English speaking educational systems is the degree of choice high school students have in selecting the subjects they study. High school students in English speaking countries may choose to study some subjects in depth, while students in most of continental Europe, including Poland, are required to study a larger number of different subjects, and will often acquire broader knowledge at the cost of depth.

Tertiary Level

Universities in Poland offer programs of study in all areas of science, social science and the humanities. They attract each year more candidates than they can take. As mentioned in Chapter 2 of this book, education became an asset in Poland, something people aspired to, and so most university departments introduced very competitive entrance examinations to ensure that only the best students filled available places. Like all educational institutions, universities had to put up with interference from the Communist authorities, not only with programs, but also in entrance requirements. For example, the ruling Communist Party gradually introduced means by which places were secured in good schools and universities for the children of party members. Especially after the riots at universities in March 1968, a system of preferences was established to this end, as well as a mechanism allowing the higher positions in the academic world to be filled by appointment. The system did not work very well, except in subjects such as philosophy, economics and 19th and 20th century Polish and Russian histories, in which the old core of professors made sure that standards of education were kept high. They did this by setting demanding examinations and failing less capable students irrespective of their parents' or their own political allegiance.

In fact, the establishment after the March 1968 riots of the appointed, associate and full professorial positions was the last ditch attempt by the party to get more of its own people into high academic positions. The attempt failed because scholars appointed in this way were generally scorned and referred to by the rest of the staff as *marcowi docenci* (the March associate professors). As a result, most genuine scholars who happened to be party members at the same time preferred to gain their positions through their scholarly pursuits rather than their political views. Thus, Polish universities do not differ much from other similar European institutions as far as the quality of education and research is concerned.

Even at university level, there was little choice available to students undertaking specialist areas of study. All the subjects were obligatory and usually included specialist subjects, a language—including at least one year of Russian—education, Marxist philosophy and economics. In contrast, universities in English speaking countries give students almost unlimited freedom to choose the subjects they wish to study in addition to their major. In Poland, the last reform of tertiary education in the late 1980s has finally removed this restriction so that even though now Polish university students still have to study a large number of specialist subjects, they also have the freedom to choose additional subjects.

The Polish tertiary education system makes a clear distinction between universities—where it takes four to five years to complete a Masters degree with a thesis and exams—and professional colleges, where students obtain diplomas qualifying them after two to four years of study for such professions as accounting, primary school teaching and as electricians. The methodology and quality of teaching in tertiary institutions does not differ significantly from other countries, except that Polish students must complete a Masters degree if they are enrolled at a university—Bachelors degrees cannot be attained in Poland.

Thus, there are significant differences between the Polish education system and education systems in English speaking countries, especially as far as the amount of factual knowledge and skills taught at primary and secondary levels is concerned. There are only formal differences (such as titles) at the tertiary level. Unfortunately, these differences have meant that qualifications are not always acknowledged. A PhD is the only mutually recognised degree, while Bachelor's degrees are considered in Poland to be incomplete tertiary education and Polish Master's degrees are usually accepted as the equivalent of a Batchelor's degree in English speaking countries.

The differences in approach at primary and high school levels are puzzling to many Poles, who question the quality of that type of education in English speaking countries. Similar achievements by tertiary students in all the countries concerned suggest that it would be extremely difficult to make a valid assessment of the values of any of the systems. There is no doubt, however, that most Poles arriving in English speaking countries have very little understanding of how the education systems work in those countries. They should be helped to understand how the systems work as soon after their arrival as practical.

> Most Polish immigrants have a negative view of the quality of school education in English speaking countries.
>
> (a) Ask your Polish students what they think are the weaknesses of the education system in your country.
> (b) What are the advantages of the educational system in English speaking countries?

Teaching of English in Poland

During most of the post-World War II period English has been the most popular foreign language in Poland, both as a school subject and as an extracurricular subject taught by private individuals, language teaching cooperatives and private schools. Both the British and the United States consular posts in Poland have helped English teachers to keep in touch with the developments by maintaining well equipped libraries, funding scholarships in England and the United States for teachers and by organising summer courses and seminars for teachers and students.

The best testimony to the quality of English teaching in Poland is the fact that only about a half of the last wave of Polish immigrants to Australia, Britain, Canada and the United States had to join elementary English courses. The other half used what English they had to find work and spent the first few years organising their lives. Many of them are only now looking for more specialised, advanced courses and are often disappointed. In fact there is at the moment a considerable number of Poles in all English speaking countries whose elementary or intermediate English acquired in Poland has carried them to the point where they need to improve it. On inquiry they find that English language teaching is directed at new arrivals, and that advanced courses are not only scarce, but are rarely designed to teach corrective grammar and the cultural and stylistic aspects of English usage. Consequently, many immigrants end up hiring a private tutor.

Finally, most Poles have been educated in a system which puts a lot of emphasis on systematic learning from a textbook and requires the student to work hard at home. Consequently, teachers who do not use textbooks but bring new sets of photocopied materials for each lesson, who do not give much homework and those who do not correct their students' grammatical mistakes are inevitably treated with suspicion and, if progress is not considered to be satisfactory, Polish students may quickly drop out from courses.

Things to Think About

1. Below is a list of commonly expressed attitudes to language learning.
   (a) Decide whether you agree or disagree with each statement.
   (b) Arrange the statements in order from those you consider to be the most important statement to the least important.
   (c) Discuss your choice of order with the rest of the class.
      (i)   Learning correct grammar is an important part of an English course.
      (ii) Learning vocabulary is an important part of an English course.
      (iii) Learning to talk in everyday situations is an important part of an English course.
      (iv) Learning to spell correctly is an important part of an English course.
      (v)   Learning to write correctly is an important part of an English course.
      (vi) It is not possible to learn English properly without a textbook.
      (vii) I feel happy when my teacher corrects my mistakes while I talk.
      (viii) I feel frustrated when my teacher corrects my mistakes while I talk.
      (ix) A thorough knowledge of grammatical rules is essential for a student to communicate effectively in English.
2. If you could make any changes you wished, what changes would you make to the way English is taught in your course?
3. (a) Do you think there are any differences in the way English is taught in Poland and the way it is taught in English speaking countries? If so, list the differences and explain them to the rest of the class.
   (b) List the strengths of each system.
   (c) Compare your list with those of other students and discuss it with the rest of the class.

CHAPTER EIGHT

VALUES IN THE POLISH SOCIETY

Polish society cherishes the same basic values as most other Western cultures, although Poland's location in Europe, its history and the temperament of its peoples have made some of these values more important than others. Consequently, a Polish person's view of the world will differ from the world view of an Australian, for example. Unfortunately, this may lead to misinterpretation of behaviour on both sides, as well as to the belief that one's own values are superior to those of others. The aim of this chapter is to give readers insight into Polish system of values, and the questions at the end of the chapter have been designed to help Poles understand the way people in English speaking countries interpret the world around them.

As mentioned above, most of the values held by English speaking and Polish societies have common roots but, as cultural differences between Americans, Australians, Britons, Canadians and New Zealanders clearly demonstrate, even the values of the people from the same stock develop differently due to historical reasons. So it is only to be expected that Polish history has influenced the values of Polish people. It is, in fact, the last 200 years of history that have influenced most values presently held by Poles. These values can be summed up in five key words, and while the values they encapsulate are shared by native speakers of English to some extent, they have gained special importance in Poland. They are: freedom, fatherland, honour, dignity and solidarity.

Freedom

It is by no accident that the concept of freedom in both the collective and the individual senses is the most important value to Poles. This is mainly because Poland has lacked freedom for much of the past 200 years, which has affected the lives of all Poles. As a state, Poland was not free from 1795 to 1919, during the German occupation from 1939 to 1945 and during the Communist rule between 1945 and 1989. As a result, the gaining and maintaining of national freedom became and remains today a major concern to all Poles.

When the partitioning of Poland was concluded in 1795, the partitioning powers themselves provided the impulse for the replacement of the older concept of loyalty towards the monarch with the modern concept of national freedom and loyalty towards the state. Soon after the last partitioning of Poland, the Austrian, Prussian and Russian emperors declared jointly that 'the Polish state had been erased from the map of Europe for ever'. In response, Poland as a state of its people rather than the domain of a monarch began to appear prominently in the 19th century writings of Polish philosophers, publicists, novelists and poets. Already in 1797, very soon after Poland lost independence, Józef Wybicki wrote a nationalistic song for the soldiers of Polish legions formed in Italy to fight alongside Napoleon's army. This later became the national anthem of independent Poland. Such nationalistic writings and other forms of peaceful resistance were accompanied by repeated armed struggles in which many Poles showed that they were ready to pay the highest price for freedom.

Another aspect of freedom that is dear to every Pole's heart is the notion that every individual has the right to initiative, originality and self-expression—that is, to personal freedom. These concepts evolved from the old notion of 'golden freedom', which referred mainly to the privileges granted by the king to the gentry during the Middle Ages and Renaissance and to the nobles' individual right to influence matters of the state and do as they pleased on their own estates. As a result of the philosophical movements of the 18th century, the last remnants of feudalism were removed with the granting of freedom to the last serfs in 1864, when significant changes in social structure—such as the collapse of the gentry class and the development of the new 'intelligentsia' class—were made. The concepts of individual freedom and of rights were considerably enriched and gradually updated, so that after independence was finally won in 1919, Poles began to play a prominent role in the political process.

Unfortunately, personal freedom was soon to be denied again, first by the Germans during World War II, then by the Communist Government between 1945 and 1989. It is actually during the latter period that the emphasis on individual freedom and, consequently, decreasing emphasis on such other important issues as the rights of women and minorities, gained strength. These issues were dealt with on paper only by the Communist Government, but the struggle to regain freedom and, in particular, the freedom to influence matters of the state, was on every Pole's mind throughout the Communist period and proved to be the main factor in abolishing the totalitarian system.

It is only to be expected then that the past 200 years of Polish history have made contemporary Poles extremely sensitive to any real or imagined threat to individual freedom. The old traditions of the age of golden freedom have added fuel to this fire, leading to suspicion of any authority and occasional tendency towards anarchy.

Fatherland

While in English the word 'motherland' is used to describe the land of one's origin, in Polish it is the word *ojczyzna* (fatherland) that is used for the same purpose. The word 'motherland' emphasises the emotional connection one has with the country of one's origins, whereas the word *ojczyzna* is a direct translation of the Latin word *patria*, which refers to one's inheritance passed from father to son. Thus the word *ojczyzna* implies not only love for one's origins, but also a strong feeling of possessiveness and the need to fight for one's inheritance—feelings which are also reflected in the word *patriotyzm* (patriotism).

As described in Chapter 2 of this book, Poles have had to fight for their very existence both on their own soil and abroad. Ever since the end of the 18th century, each generation has paid with their lives to achieve the seemingly unachievable: independence for the fatherland. This attitude is well characterised by a popular Polish saying, *Miłe blizny dla ojczyzny* (The scars received for the fatherland are honourable).

Thus *ojczyzna* is central to Polish life. It is a word that is frequently used in everyday conversations, which used to often revolve around the various attempts at independence. Now that full territorial and political independence has been regained, the word *ojczyzna* still has a unique meaning to Poles, a holy quality like an altar or the grave of a freedom fighter.

Honour

Like the nobility in other European cultures, Polish aristocracy observed an internationally accepted code of honour which, at the same time, had some typically Polish peculiarities. It consisted of a set of principles concerning social etiquette, especially concerned with offensive behaviour and reactions to it. It also emphasised principles of honesty and honourable dealings with other nobility.

There is one significant difference between Polish and other European cultures in this regard. In Poland, the classes who traditionally observed the code of honour collapsed after 1864 because many nobles lost their lands as a punishment for participating in the January 1864 uprising. The nobles who remained were decimated by the effects of the industrial revolution which taking place in Poland at the time. They were gradually integrated into other social groups, particularly the intelligentsia, which inherited from the nobility the code of honour along with many other traditional values. Unlike the aristocracy and the gentry, however, the intelligentsia was not a closed social class since it was no longer birth alone that qualified a person to be a member of that class.

This process of social change continued during the Communist period so that today practically the whole of Polish society has embraced and modified the code, which has been adapted to suit the contemporary situation. Consequently, most Poles consider it very important to have a good image of themselves, and they tend to ostracise people who have through dishonourable conduct lost face. They are careful to observe proper etiquette, and *Słowo honoru* (word of honour), like other matters of honour, is treated very seriously indeed.

Finally, there has always been a connection between honour, patriotism and fatherland, which is best expressed in this ancient call of the Polish gentry: *Za honor i ojczyznę!* (In the name of honour and the fatherland!), which today can still incite Poles to incredible feats of bravery and sacrifice if used by the right person in a worthy cause for Poland.

Dignity

It seems that only the Nazis surpassed the Communists in depriving Poles of dignity, although documents that are only now coming to light may prove that both powers occupy an equal place in the black pages of Polish history. Poles were not only humiliated by being ruled by a government imposed by a foreign power, they were also mistreated by the state security service and other law enforcement institutions, as well as by uneducated party bullies at local level. This, together with poverty—which affected everyone except highly placed party officials—deprived Poles of a sense of pride and dignity. To compensate, Poles carried themselves in an exceedingly proud manner, bearing poverty and other difficulties with dignity and honour. It was important for them to dress well, acquire knowledge and maintain contact with cultural developments outside Poland. In short, keeping up the sophisticated appearance of dignity became a way of life.

The younger generation were taught by their elders to observe similar good manners and to be decent in their dealings with other people. They also imitated their elders by devoting a lot of time and energy to decorating their small flats fashionably. Even people who could not afford to entertain friends at home would invite them for a cup of coffee, which would sometimes be served with only one biscuit for each person, but on the best china available and with elegant silver spoons. This would always be accompanied by pleasant, often refined conversation on all manner of subjects.

One of the most apparent manifestations of these attitudes is the way Poles dress. Women especially show great ingenuity in acquiring fashionable clothes. Seamstresses in Poland are kept well occupied, and Western fashion magazines, such as the German *Burda* which has dressmaking patterns in it, sell very quickly, since many women sew their own and their families' clothes.

Of all the English speaking nations, Americans and Australians seem to be most casual about the way they dress, which often leads Poles arriving in those countries to make the false assumption that most people are either very poor or they simply do not care about the way they look. In a recent survey of newly arrived Polish immigrants (Gebauer 1992), Australians way of dressing was almost unanimously seen as a negative aspect of the country and its people. This is clearly reflected in some of the comments made by people participating in the survey. One woman remembered thinking, 'These people cannot even afford proper shoes!' Other typical comments were, 'It makes no difference whether a person is rich or poor, if somebody is well dressed they are not Australian!', and 'It is impossible to judge a person's social standing from his everyday appearance here'.

Finally, while everyone in Poland is happy to accept gifts or unexpected bonuses, people are extremely sensitive about accepting any form of charity. The way help is given, especially financial or material assistance, to those Poles who need it is very important because it will determine whether help will be accepted and whether the person receiving it is going to be a friend or not. Having had to keep up appearances in their home country, most Poles will gratefully accept charity abroad only if they are not humiliated in the process.

Solidarity

It is pertinent that the movement which eventually brought about the collapse of the Communist Government in Poland was called Solidarity. During the past five decades the lack of support for the government, together with the general poverty of the population has led to a revival of traditional family values and close friendships. It has also facilitated the development of a network of groups within the society, which support each other in ways somewhat similar to the extended family. In other words, a sense of solidarity, of 'us' against 'them', was very strong, a feeling upon which the Solidarity movement drew heavily when it was formed in 1980.

As a result of this, contemporary Poles attach great importance to family ties and bonds of friendship, which they consider to be a sort of personal asset. Furthermore, family and group solidarity has become not just something that can be expected within a family or circle of friends; it is also a duty. Moreover, people who wilfully fail to live up to these expectations are treated unfavourably, irrespective of whether they are extended family members or friends. In the case of family, individuals who fail in their duties will be ostracised by the family by not being invited to important occasions and being deprived of information shared by family members. Having meted out punishment, the family will, however, accept apologies and welcome the prodigal son or daughter to its bosom in the hope that the lesson had been learnt and the lack of family responsibility will not be repeated.

Close friendships and ties developed within support groups are based on principles similar to the code of honour and often last a lifetime. People who belong to such groups usually maintain close contacts, have similar information lines to those of a family and frequently perform favours for each other. If members of the group find themselves in serious trouble, they can usually count on help either from individuals in the group or from the group as a whole.

Ties such as these survive even when there is no direct contact for a long time, for instance, when a member of such a group emigrates to a distant country. In fact, members of the group may expect to be assisted by the fortunate member living in another country, or even sponsored for emigration into that country. However, unlike the family, such groups rarely forgive members who seriously breach the unwritten code of practice. Rather, the person responsible will be permanently ostracised by all members of the group.

Even though life in a developed country allows individuals to take care of themselves and does not necessitate such close ties, Polish immigrants are used to having their family and a group of close friends around them, and therefore strongly feel their absence. If asked whether there is a single most painful aspect of immigration, most Poles reply without any hesitation that it is the loss of direct contact with family and friends and hence the loss of strong sense of security based on their support in difficult times.

1. In this chapter some key words have been used to describe important Polish values. What similar words represent the values of your culture? List as many of these as you can.
2. To what extent do you think these values are reflected in the education system?

Things to Think About

1. Many important Polish values and attitudes can be expressed by words such as *wolność, ojczyzna, honor, rodzina* and *przyjaźń.*
   (a) Identify a similar list of key values relating to an English speaking culture.
   (b) Choose two or three of these values and explain why you think they are important.
   (c) How do you think these values are practised in everyday life? Give some examples.
   (d) Do your English speaking friends agree with your list? Why/why not?
2. Ask two or three of your friends from one English speaking country to nominate an object that best represents their country.
   (a) Ask them to explain why they think this object represents their country.
   (b) Compare your findings with those of other people in your class.
   (c) What do the objects nominated suggest about the culture of that country as a whole?

CHAPTER NINE

TĘSKNOTA
Culture Shock Revisited

As discussed in Chapter 1 of this book, most immigrants go through the experience of cultural shock. They feel disoriented, frustrated and helpless, needing a period of adjustment to overcome the difficulties and learn to cope in the new environment. However, for many Poles this is not where uncomfortable or unhappy feelings about immigration end. Many go through recurrent periods of feeling a sense of loss and lingering doubts about whether their decision to emigrate was right. These feelings are due to lack of direct contact with their friends and relatives in Poland, with their familiar, rich, cultural tradition and with Polish landscapes which they had grown to love. In short, they keenly miss the fatherland.

Polish uses the word *tęsknota* to describe this feeling, which cannot be directly translated into English. In *The Great Dictionary of the Polish Language* the word *tęsknota* is defined as:

> . . . a feeling caused by separation with someone (something) close to one's heart, the urge to return to someone (something) that one has not seen for a long time, to someone (something) lost.

While English has a number of words that refer to the effects of separation or not being able to reach something or someone for various reasons—such as 'missing', 'longing for', 'yearning for' and 'homesickness'—which are most often used to translate *tęsknota* into English, neither the individual words nor any of their combinations reflect adequately the full meaning of the Polish word. The same concept does not exist in English language cultures.

While *tęsknota* can refer to people and things in Poland, the concept is usually associated with people separated from their loved ones or things by obstacles which are difficult to overcome. These include state borders—which during the partition included the borders between Russian, Prussian and Austrian-occupied Poland—and great distances. It is most often associated with people who were either forced to emigrate for political reasons or emigrated voluntarily to a far away place.

In the case of political exiles, *tęsknota* is justified and understandable. Most immigrants, however, are economic immigrants and, after the first difficult years, usually fare much better in the host country than they did in Poland. What then is their *tęsknota* about?

The answer is a complex one. Generally speaking, it is an individual thing which is difficult to describe. It is probably best explained by the Polish romantic poet, Cyprian Kamil Norwid who, while in exile in Paris, wrote the poem 'My Song' describing this feeling. While reading the poem (below), you may like to play a recording of Frederick Chopin's (also a Polish political exile) *Nocturne Opus 37 No 1 in C-sharp Minor*.

My Song (II)
i. For that land where people raise a crumb of bread from the ground out of respect for the gifts of Heaven . . .
    I yearn, O Lord.
ii. For that land where it is a great offence to destroy a stork's nest in its pear-tree, because storks are of use to all . . .
    I yearn, O Lord.
iii. For that land where greetings are like an eternal confession of God: 'Praised be Jesus Christ!' . . .
    I yearn, O Lord.
iv. I yearn for yet one other thing, but I know not where lies its home, a thing equally innocent . . .
    I yearn, O Lord.
v. For no-yearning, for no-thinking, for those who hold yea for yea—nay for nay, without lights and shades,
    I yearn, O Lord.
vi. I yearn for the place where there is—who to heed me?
    Such there must be, though it shall not so happen to my desire.
                    (translation by M.A. Michael in Filip & Michael 1944)

While similar feelings may be experienced from time to time by all immigrants, Poles share with their eastern Slavic neighbours a tendency that is well illustrated by some of the heroes created by the great Russian novelist Dostoyevski. Basically, it is a tendency to probe deeply and passionately into one's spiritual wounds, resulting in repeated, prolonged periods of suffering.

The symptoms of suffering caused by *tęsknota* are very similar to those caused by cultural shock. Depending on the individual's personality, it will demonstrate itself by apathy, irritability, negative attitudes to or withdrawal from the host country's culture and nationals and sometimes heavy drinking.

Since there are no exhaustive studies of the phenomenon, we will have to leave open the question of whether *tęsknota* is simply an occasional manifestation of culture shock or something peculiarly Polish. As with this book, *tęsknota* and related feelings might be a suitable subject of discussion with students to conclude an intercultural component of a course.

REFERENCES

Brick, Jean (1991), *China: A Handbook in Intercultural Communication*, National Centre for English Language Teaching and Research, Macquarie University, Sydney.

Clyne, Michael (1991), *Community Languages: The Australian Experience*, Cambridge University Press, Melbourne.

Corder, P.S. (1973), *Introducing Applied Linguistics*, Penguin Books, Baltimore.

Davies, Norman (1985), *God's Playground: A History of Poland*, vols 1 & 2, Clarendon Press, Oxford.

Filip, T.M. & Michael, M.A. (1944), *A Polish Anthology*, Duckworth, London.

Gebauer, Vivian (unpub.), *A Contrastive Analysis of Selected Polish and Australian Communication Patterns*, Department of Polish Studies, Macquarie University, Sydney.

Kalantzis, Mary, Cope, Bill & Slade, Diana (1986), *The Language Question. The Maintenance of Languages Oher Than English*, vol. 1, Australian Government Publishing Service, Canberra.

Klos Sokol, Laura (1994), *Speaking Volumes About Poles*, International Publishing Services, Warsaw.

O'Grady, K. & Moore, M. (1994), *Finding Common Ground: Crosscultural Communication Strategies For Job Seekers*, National Centre for English Language Teaching and Research, Macquarie University, Sydney.

Pakulski, Jan (1985), 'Polish Migrants in Hobart: A Study of Community Formation', in Sussex, R. & Zubrzycki, J. (eds) *Polish People and Culture in Australia*, Department of Demography, Institute of Advanced Studies, Australian National University, Canberra, pp. 82–107.

Smolicz, Jerzy & Secombe, M.J. (1985). 'Polish Culture and Education in Australia: A Review of Some Recent Research and Educational Developments', in Sussex, R. & Zubrzycki, J. (eds), *Polish People and Culture in Australia*, Department of Demography, Institute of Advanced Studies, Australian National University, Canberra.

Suchodolski, Bogdan (1987), Dzieje kultury Polskiej, 2nd edn, Polska Agencja Wydawnicza Interpress, Warszawa.

Walicki, Andrzej (1990), 'The Three Traditions in Polish Patriotism' in: Gomulka, S. & Polonsky, A. (eds), *Polish Paradoxes*, Routledge, London, pp. 21–39.

Wierzbicka, Anna (1985), 'The Double Life of a Bilingual', in Sussex, R. & Zubrzycki, J. (eds), *Polish People and Culture in Australia*, Department of Demography, Institute of Advanced Studies, Australian National University, Canberra, pp. 187–223.

BIBLIOGRAPHY

General

Bąk, Piotr (979), *Gramatyka Języka Polskiego*, Wiedza Powszechna, Warszawa.

Brick, Jean (1991), *China: A Handbook in Intercultural Communication*, National Centre for English Language Teaching and Research, Macquarie University, Sydney.

Clyne, Michael (1991), *Community Languages: The Australian Experience*, Cambridge University Press, Melbourne.

Corder P.S. (1973), *Introducing Applied Linguistics*, Penguin Books, Baltimore.

Czaplinski, Wladyslaw & Tadeusz, Ladogorski (eds) (1993), *Atlas HIstoryczny Polski*, Polskie Przedsiebiorstwo Wydawnictw Kartograficznych S.A., Warszawa-Wroclaw.

Czarnecka Urszula (1990), *Nauczanie mówienia wjęzyku Polskim jako rozwijanie kompetencji komunikacyjnej* (program dydaktyczny), Instytut Badań Polonijnych, Uniwersytet Jagielloński, Kraków.

Czubinski, Antoni & Jerzy, Topolski (1989), *Historia Polski*, Ossolineum, Wroclaw.

Davies, Norman (1985), *God's Playground: A History of Poland*, vols 1 & 2, Clarendon Press, Oxford.

Gebauer, Vivian (unpub.), *A Contrastive Analysis of Selected Polish and Australian Communication Patterns*, Department of Polish Studies, Macquarie University, Sydney.

Janicki, Karol (1985), *The Foreigner's Language: A Sociolinguistic Perspective*, Pergamon Press, Oxford.

Kalantzis, Mary, Cope, Bill & Slade, Diana (1986), *The Language Question: The Maintenance of Languages Other Than English*, vol. 1, Australian Government Publishing Service, Canberra.

Klos Sokol, Laura (1994): *Speaking Volumes About Poles*, International Publishing Services, Warsaw.

Pakulski, Jan (1985), 'Polish Migrants in Hobart: A Study of Community Formation', in Sussex, R. and Zubrzycki, J. (eds) *Polish People and Culture in Australia*, Department of Demography, Institute of Advanced Studies, Australian National University, Canberra, pp. 82–107.

Smolicz, Jerzy & Secombe, M.J. (1985). 'Polish Culture and Education in Australia: A Review of Some Recent Research and Educational Developments', in Sussex, R. & Zubrzycki, J. (eds), *Polish People and Culture in Australia*, Department of Demography, Institute of Advanced Studies, Australian National University, Canberra.

Van Ek, J.A. & Alexander, L.G. (1988), *Threshold Level English*, Council of Europe Modern Language Project, Prentice Hall, London.

Walicki, Andrzej (1990), 'The Three Traditions in Polish Patriotism' in Gomulka, S. & Polonsky, A. (eds), *Polish Paradoxes*, Routledge, London, pp. 21–39.

Wierzbicka, Anna (1985), 'The Double Life of a Bilingual', in Sussex, R. & Zubrzycki, J. (eds), *Polish People and Culture in Australia*, Department of Demography, Institute of Advanced Studies, Australian National University, Canberra, pp. 187–223.

Poland and Polish culture

Barnett, Clifford R. (1958), *Poland, Its People, Its Society, Its Culture*, Hraf Press, New Haven.

Filip, T.M. & Michael, M.A. (1944), *A Polish Anthology*, Duckworth, London.

Gomulka, S. & Polonsky, A. (eds) (1990), *Polish Paradoxes*, Routledge, London.

Halecki, Oskar & Polonsky, A. (1983) *The History of Poland*. Routledge & Henley, London.

Leslie, R.F. (ed.) (1980), *The History of Poland Since 1863*, Cambridge University Press, Cambridge.

Milosz, Czeslaw (1983), *The History of Polish Literature*, University of California Press, Los Angeles.

Paszkowski, Lech (1987), *Poles in Australia and Oceania 1740–1940*, Australian National University Press, Canberra.

Skurnowicz, Joan S. (1981), 'Romantic Nationalism and Liberalism', *Joachim Lelewel and the Polish National Idea*, East European Monographs, no. 83, Columbia University Press.

Suchodolski, Bogdan (1987), *Dzieje kultury Polskiej*, 2nd edn, Polska Agencja Wydawnicza Interpress, Warszawa.

Sussex, R. & Zubrzycki, J. (eds) (1985), *Polish People and Culture in Australia*, Department of Demography, Institute of Advanced Studies, Australian National University, Canberra.

Swan, Oscar (1980), *A Concise Grammar of Polish*, Orbis Books Ltd, London.

Wierzbicka, Anna (1985), 'The Double Life of a Bilingual', in Sussex, R. & Zubrzycki, J. (eds) *Polish People and Culture in Australia*, Department of Demography, Institute of Advanced Studies, Australian National University, Canberra, pp 187–223.

Zagorska Brooks, Maria (1975), *Polish Reference Grammar*, Mouton, Paris.

Zamoyski, Adam (1987) *The Polish Way*, John Murray Publishers, London.

Reading for English language students

Clark, Manning (1992), *A Short History of Australia*, Pengiun, Melbourne.

Kearney, Hugh (1989), *The British Isles: A History of Four Nations*, Cambridge University Press, Cambridge.

Quirk, Randolf (1985) *A Comprehensive Grammar of the English Language*, Longman, London.

—— (1990), *English in Use*, Longman, London.

Tindall, George B. (1992), *America: A Narrative History*, Norton, New York.

Willis D (1991), *Collins COBUILD Student's Grammar*, Harper Collins, London.